Intimate Marketing

By

Gil Peretz

Intimate Marketing

Social Networking is *Not* Enough:
How to Make Customers Love You Forever!

By

Gil Peretz

Intimate Marketing

Social Networking is Not Enough:
How to Make Customers Love You Forever!

Copyright © 2011 Gil Peretz

All rights reserved.

ISBN: 1456506374

ISBN-13: 978-1-4565-0637-7

Library of Congress Control Number: 2011900316

CreateSpace, North Charleston, SC

For translation rights please contact rights@Intimatemarketing.com
To explore the possibilities of bringing International speaker Gil Peretz to your
organization, contact gil@gilperetz.com

Printed in the United States of America

Dedication

To Nili

*who taught me so much about
the power of my words*

A Personal Confession, or Why is This Book Worth Reading?

Is this book a story? Is it for business people and managers? Is it also a romance novel, of all things? Yes. Why write it this way? People love stories. People remember stories.

As an international speaker, I have discovered the power of stories. If a picture is worth a thousand words, then a story is worth a thousand pictures. Every year, I speak in front of many organizations around the world, and stories work for all cultures.

When you hear a story, you connect with your 'right brain,' you activate your imagination, and the images in the story do the work for you. "Adults are just little kids in big bodies." This quote from training guru Robert Pike explains why we love stories at any age. From the time we are born, we hear stories. They bring enjoyment, and, as a by-product, they expand our mental abilities.

I got the idea to write this book after reading a few of Dr. Ken Blanchard's books, including *The One-Minute Manager*. I looked for a way to convey the concepts that would make everyone enjoy him or herself, but the main thing was to make them remember the concepts of "Intimate Marketing."

This book constitutes a "first" in the world: a marketing novel. It may not be the best *novel* you've ever read or will read. Nevertheless, if you look closely at what people remember after reading ordinary books on marketing and management, you will find that they remember very little. Most of us remember one model, one table, an acronym, and perhaps a story or joke.

Intimate Marketing is a different kind of book. I guarantee that you will no longer forget the way to attract, and keep, customers, or how to use the theory of contact called the *Kama Sutra* of marketing. In short, you will remember how to relate in a different way to your customers.

Who knows? Maybe next year, instead of preparing a "marketing plan," you'll prepare a plan entitled, "A Love Story Strategy with Our Customers."

Intimate Marketing gives you, in an experiential way, the tools to get the result every business expects to achieve: more profits.

The one Intimate Marketing principle is regular feedback from each contact. Therefore, if you like the book, then send me a 'love letter,' revealing your opinions and telling me what you liked (and, more importantly, what you applied after reading the book).

Please send your letter, together with some details about yourself, to gil@gilperetz.com or visit me at www. IntimateMarketing.com

Yours,
Gil Peretz
International Speaker and Author

P.S. A large part of Intimate Marketing can be applied not only to contacts with customers, but also with employees, bosses, partners, and suppliers. Reading this *novel* is the start of your personal journey. You are invited to add your own "soul" and style in applying it.

Contents

Chapter 1: The Bait 1

Chapter 2: What is I.N.T.I.M.A.T.E.?. 9

Chapter 3: The Rendezvous. 31

Chapter 4: Business before Pleasure 51

Chapter 5: Love in the Mirror 67

Chapter 6: Intimacy in Marketing 79

Chapter 7: Kama Sutra 89

Chapter 8: Contact 99

Chapter 9: It's About Love... 119

Chapter 10: Forever Faithful 131

Epilogue 137

Afterword 139

Gil Peretz. 141

Recommendations from Linkedin ®. 145

Chapter 1

The Bait

*E*laine was at her desk studying her iPad, when suddenly, she struck her forehead in self-reproach. Three days from now, the iPad reminded her, was Robert's birthday. Damn! Her closest friend since fourth grade and she still hadn't gotten him anything for his birthday. Now she understood why he had insisted she book a seat on the flight to Acapulco with him in exactly three days. *Great,* she thought, *he found his* own *way of celebrating his thirtieth birthday!*

After several minutes, an idea occurred to her about how she might really surprise him. She made a mental note to call the airline first thing the next morning. As a platinum member of the International Airlines' (IA) Frequent Flyer program, she could expect some special favors—although not, of course, like Robert could expect. His frequent trips to Europe and the Far East had earned him far more frequent flyer points than even *she* had accumulated.

When she made the call to International Airlines, the CSR–the customer service representative–was pleasant enough. Although, after identifying herself as a platinum customer, he refused to grant her unusual request. She had asked them to deliver a personal gift to her friend, Robert, wishing him a "happy birthday, from Elaine."

"Who is responsible for marketing your Frequent Flyer program?" she inquired, her voice heavy with disappointment. "Daniel Marks," answered the CSR. "But he's on vacation. He won't be back until next week."

* * *

When Daniel Marks returned from his week-long vacation at a remote cabin in the Alps, he found waiting for him on his desk the inevitable pile of mail. One envelope, with its round swirls on a pastel purple background stood out from all the rest. He opened that one first. *My name is Elaine Sherman,* the letter began after addressing him personally, *and I hope you enjoyed your vacation. You don't know me and we have never spoken, although I have been a Frequent Flyer member for three years now. I manage a successful consulting company. Since I am something of a marketing expert, I am inviting you to attend one of my seminars in two weeks, on Thursday September 3 at 6:00 p.m., at the New York Marriott Marquis, 1535 Broadway, New York. I will not elaborate at this time, but based on a chance conversation I had with one of your staff members, allow me to say that you really should attend this seminar.*

Daniel's first thought was that this Elaine Sherman, whoever she was, had a lot of nerve. Talk about coming on strong. Afterwards, he turned on his computer, typed her name, and immediately saw that she actually did have quite an impressive flying record with IA. In vain, he searched for some kind of personal information about her. Aside from her birth date, social security number, and phone numbers, the computer revealed nothing about her that would distinguish her from the long list of customers. He googled her name and found that she was mentioned in hundreds of articles. She had a unique website and more than forty-two hundred friends on Facebook.

By this time, Daniel was extremely curious about her. Before he opened any more mail, he noted the date and location of Elaine's seminar in his calendar. "Maybe I can just slip in without anyone knowing who I am," he muttered to himself.

* * *

Elaine Sherman sat in her pleasant, spacious office, wondering if Daniel Marks would really attend her seminar. She had learned the presentation material by heart long ago. Although she hadn't actually invented the concept, she had lectured about it on many occasions. She enjoyed speaking about the 'Intimate Marketing revolution' because, as a thirty-year-old woman, she had benefited financially by following its principles. For her, it had proven its validity long ago.

Shortly before six o'clock on the evening of the seminar, dozens of people congregated in the Marriott lobby. Elaine was making some final preparations in the SoHo meeting room before admitting the participants. At the same time, Daniel was parking his new GMC Acadia in the hotel parking lot. For good measure, he straightened his tie and applied a little more of Armani's

Acqua di Gio, just in case Elaine Sherman or some other woman showed relationship potential. When you're thirty-four, single, and watching all your friends getting married and raising families, there's no sense in passing up an opportunity.

At the meeting room entrance, a hostess was graciously requesting that all participants record their names and a few personal details on her list. Daniel Marks hesitated momentarily, but then decided to list his full name, since no one would be reviewing the list until after the seminar, at which time he would be long gone. When Erica, one of Elaine's assistants, noticed the name Dan Marks on the list, she smiled slightly, excused herself for a moment, and walked off seemingly toward the restrooms. But at the last minute, she slipped into the meeting room to give Elaine a triumphant 'thumbs-up' sign. Elaine smiled broadly in return. She was now ready to begin her quest: to completely transform Daniel Marks' marketing philosophy, and perhaps his life as well.

The lights dimmed to a soft glow. Music by *Enigma* filled the air in the packed lecture hall. Elaine stepped up to the speaker's platform, with a lit candle in her hand, and announced, "Today we will be discussing Intimate Marketing." She extinguished the candle, and then the lights were returned to their normal level. Daniel Marks was surprised. First, the unconventional introduction caught his attention. Second, he had to admit that the pantsuit Elaine was wearing really made quite an impression. No, she was not at all what he had imagined.

"Intimate Marketing constitutes an upgrade to the next level of what has been known as 'Permission Marketing,'" Elaine continued.

Daniel liked the word 'upgrade'; at International Airlines, upgrading was definitely one of the common buzzwords. Although he felt a bit out of his element, like someone undergoing hypnosis, he really didn't mind.

"Intimate Marketing successfully integrates the two 'hottest' marketing topics of the twenty-first century: CRM, or Customer Relationship Management, and social networks. Intimate Marketing is based on relationship development via a contact system whose success lies in a genuine understanding between two parties: the marketing company and the customer or client. The associations that come to mind as one considers the word 'intimate' are also appropriate for this discussion. In Intimate Marketing the company attempts to get to know the customers from every possible angle. Management is interested in finding out what the customer likes, when and how he or she likes it, how often, and why."

Daniel loved the analogies.

Elaine descended from the platform and continued her lecture as she strolled among the tables, stopping periodically to address those seated at the one nearest her. "In order to develop and preserve an intimate relationship with a customer, the company must attempt to identify, meet, and exceed each person's needs by capturing and studying as much information as possible about them. Just as the needs of a married couple change over time, so do those of the customer. Circumstances are constantly changing. An effective marketer must be able to identify and respond quickly to changes. Most importantly, they must know how to meet their clients' needs at the proper time. If you are providing exactly what your customer wants and needs, he or she will be an enthusiastic and willing participant in building a stronger relationship, so that the level of intimacy will grow naturally."

In his innermost thoughts, Daniel was forced to acknowledge that he was eagerly devouring every word Elaine Sherman uttered. However, at times, the imagery she occasionally evoked sent his thoughts off in other, decidedly intimate directions. He noticed that Elaine had begun to reverse the typical order of references from 'he or she' in her lecture, to 'she or he.' Doing so drew Daniel's attention to *Elaine's* personal needs. Was that intentional...? What if, as the seminar ended, some tall, handsome young man approached Elaine, took her by the hand, picked up her briefcase, and escorted her to her car? He hoped fervently that this would not be the case. Suddenly, he felt a strong desire to find out if Elaine was unattached and available. What a shame that there were no details provided in IA's Frequent Flyer program database. And that there were no clues about her personal status on her Facebook page.

Elaine smoothed back a wisp of hair and continued developing and presenting her *intimacy* theories. "What forms the basis of a good relationship between couples?" she asked. She then promptly answered, "Faithfulness. A satisfied partner, one whose needs are being met, is faithful to the other. But in addition, a satisfied customer will not only be loyal to the company she or he buys from, but will tell others about the satisfying relationship. It's a fact that the most effective advertising, by far, is word of mouth, from one satisfied customer to another. In our connected society, it has more impact than only a few years ago. People like to buy products and services that are like those which their friends buy. People like to like people like themselves, and they share their experiences of the services they have bought. When they share their thoughts on Facebook and other web-based social networks, all their friends are affected. The satisfied customer never 'betrays you.' That is, she or he never leaves you for your competition. A satisfied customer prefers to give you as much business as possible, which is called 'share of customer,' increasing their enjoyment from the relationship. They know you will not only anticipate their needs, but will also always meet, and often exceed, their expectations."

Daniel scribbled a note to himself about the idea of 'share of customer.' He wondered, however, what the connection was between this idea and 'market share.'

Elaine paused for a few seconds and lowered her voice, which immediately caused the already-attentive audience to pay even closer attention. "In a good relationship, couples talk things out when something is bothering one of them; this also applies to Intimate Marketing. It's very important for the customer to know that she can express dissatisfaction or make a complaint, and that her words will fall on concerned ears. Intimate Marketing has an efficient and open two-way communication system, the goal of which is to convey information in both directions. This can only improve a relationship over time." This time she had dropped the masculine pronoun completely. Though a small detail missed by most members of the audience, it was not lost on Daniel.

Chapter 2

What is I.N.T.I.M.A.T.E.?

laine took a deep breath as she picked up her handouts from the podium and began distributing them among the audience. Daniel sensed a tiny smile on Elaine's lips sent his way as she handed out the pale purple sheets of paper with which he was already familiar. It seemed that her gaze lingered on him for a fraction of a second before moving on to the next person. Or maybe it was just his imagination. He hoped it wasn't. *Perception is ninety-nine percent of reality,* was the phrase that came to mind from a past seminar on business creativity. Regarding Elaine Sherman, his interest in her was much stronger than he had thought possible.

Daniel looked at the pages she had handed him. The lead-in at the top of the first page began with, "What kind of an intimate relationship is the customer experiencing from the company providing the goods or services?" Following was a detailed list in smaller print.

Elaine asked one of the participants at the center table to read the text aloud.

1: INDIVIDUALITY

Your spouse wants reassurance from you that she or he is special to you. Likewise, in Intimate Marketing, the customer wants to feel that same reassurance. Naturally, this doesn't mean the company must terminate all relationships with other customers, any more than one would be expected to end all friendships after getting married. But, in order to develop and maintain an Intimate Marketing relationship, you must be sure to communicate with your customers in a way that makes them feel that they are unique and special.

Elaine asked the reader to pause. She thanked him and handed him two tickets to Madonna's upcoming Kabbalah concert as a way of saying thank you. The onlookers were stunned. *A seminar that's not only stimulating, but full of surprises, too,* Daniel thought.

Next, she asked everyone in the audience to take notes. "Please write down the following questions so you can refer to them later. One: Who are your most valuable customers, the ones with whom you would like to develop Intimate Marketing relationships? Two: What procedures, if any, do you have in place for identifying and meeting their individual needs? Are all of your employees aware of and using these systems?"

She then asked with a wide smile, "Who would like to volunteer to read next?" At least two or three hands were raised at each table. Daniel grinned. Of course! Everyone wants prizes! What an easy way to stimulate involvement and get the adrenaline flowing! *Adults are babies in big bodies; give them some presents and they're all yours.* His thoughts were cut short as a woman at his own table began to read the second of eight points listed on the handouts.

2: NURTURING

In successful love relationships, partners support, protect, and celebrate one another, taking great care to nurture each other and strengthen their union. The philosophy is, the more support and strength you give to your partner, the better able you will be to withstand future challenges together.

Ken Blanchard, coauthor of the book Whale Done! The Power of Positive Relationships, tells people to "catch people doing things right" and "don't wait until people do things exactly right before you praise them." We can—and should—adopt his insights to marketing.

Nurturing doesn't always mean responding to your partner's needs. It can also mean anticipating them and offering suggestions to simplify life. Consider the following example:

One British cellular telecom company nurtures by identifying and meeting customer needs even before the customer realizes there is a need! How do they do it? With 'Program First,' a unique and efficient way of ensuring each customer has the lowest possible billing rate. Every quarter, each customer receives, along with his/her bill, an easy-to-read table identifying all programs and associated costs offered by the company. If a customer's quarterly usage varies to the extent that a different program from the one in which she or he is enrolled would have been more cost effective, the company will issue a retroactive credit on the customer's account. The credit will be based upon the difference between the current quarterly bill and the amount the customer would have been charged had she or he been enrolled in a program better suited to his/her usage.

"So you see," continued Elaine, "this company nurtures its customers in three ways. First, they provide several programs to meet the varied needs of their customers. Second, they are flexible enough to adapt to the changing needs of *each* customer from one period to the next. Third, and perhaps most importantly, the customer doesn't need to ask for the better rate. Instead, this company takes a proactive approach and provides the discount without any question at all. That's what I call nurturing your customers! When people feel nurtured, they begin to trust those who are nurturing, which brings me to our next point…"

"What about a prize for the reader?" someone called out, preventing Elaine from continuing. Elaine answered, "You're absolutely right. Let's give her a hand and nurture her," and then she produced a bouquet of flowers from beneath her podium, handing them to the woman. Daniel was impressed. *Stimulating,* he thought, *and creative too!*

"Who will be the next reader?" Elaine asked. A young gentleman enthusiastically raised his hand and Elaine signaled for him to begin reading.

3: TRUSTWORTHINESS

To create an effective Intimate Marketing culture, the company must demonstrate trustworthiness to the customer without compromise. The company must stand behind its promises 100 percent, remaining faithful to its vow to consider the customer first. This of course means delivering the most reliable and high quality goods and services in order to meet or exceed customer expectations, and never, ever violating customer trust. For example, customer information must be treated as highly confidential and should never be made available to outside parties. In the era of the Internet-based world, confidentiality is everything, just like in love.

Elaine asked the reader to pause momentarily, and said, "Let me share with you an actual example. For a number of years now, people have been talking about 'one-to-one marketing.' The Net provides an excellent opportunity for this, because a system of 'intimate' messages can be sent using an automatic message generator. Every respectable company takes care to assure its Internet customers of their strict confidentiality, even when asked to provide their customer list to others. For reliable organizations, providing access to confidential customer information is out of the question. The extent of 'sharing' ends with allowing messages to be sent to a purchased mailing list. This way, there is no invasion of privacy. In truly intimate relationships, 'trust is a must.'

"Let's proceed to the next component of the model." She instructed her volunteer to continue reading.

4: INTERACTIVE INVOLVEMENT

*So far, we've discussed honoring, nurturing and trusting **between** partners. The key word here is **between**—which implies the involved interaction of two people in a relationship.*

An interactive partnership is never limited to a mutual exchange of honor, care, or trust. It expands to include much, much more. Successful relationships withstand the pressures of life, because each partner has something to offer, and each partner takes the other seriously by listening and learning. When we stop learning, we stop living. Therefore, when businesses refuse to listen to and learn from their customers, they are, in effect, jeopardizing their likelihood of success.

The customer is always teaching through his/her praise, complaints, and behavior. The more you listen to the customer's 'lessons,' the better you will know him or her. The more you remember the details of each lesson, and respond accordingly, the more emotionally invested and involved the customer becomes. When customers provide feedback, and witness that feedback translated into a new product or service, they become committed to and involved with the company. This element of Intimate Marketing requires companies to develop a 'learning relationship system' whereby customers are the 'teachers' imparting knowledge to be applied by 'students' (the company).

"Many years ago," Elaine said. "A famous telecommunication company, capitalizing on the fact that most long distance calls are made to a select group of friends and family members, introduced its 'Friends & Family' plan through which each customer identified the specific names and phone numbers most frequently called. As a member of this plan, discounts were awarded each time one of those designated numbers was dialed. In addition, if members enrolled those on their specific 'friends and family' list, both members benefited from an additional discount. Once enrolled, members had invested in the program. Therefore leaving would not only impact themselves, but all of their designated friends and family members too.

"Based on this example, you can see that interactive involvement is a constant give-and-take. The company listens to, responds to, and invests in the customer by meeting his or her needs. In turn, the customer invests in the company. The investment of time and money is bilateral. Don't forget that in our social network and Facebook-land era, feedback is 'speedback.' Waste no time in listening to your customers, enlisting their involvement, responding to their 'teachings' and strengthening the mutual commitment to the relationship."

Elaine paused for a moment to give the volunteer a large bag of peanut M&M's and said, "You can share this prize with your group. The interactions with your customers are very important, because the more they interact with you, the more they feel committed to you.

"Robert Cialdini, one of the world experts on influence said it simply: "People want to be consistent with their commitments. The more time your customers invest in your relationship with them, the more they will be loyal and committed."

"This concludes our session on involved interaction." Elaine selected another reader from the table on the right to read the next point.

5: MUTUAL BENEFIT
Both the company and the customer should benefit from their union. The customer should find it easier and more convenient to do business with your company, instead of the competition because of your ongoing intimate relationship. That means you must offer maximum convenience in a way that makes both customer and company appreciate the benefit.

Elaine stopped and asserted, "If you develop a 'learning relationship system' with each one of your key customers, as described in the previous section, you will create a mutually beneficial relationship that your competition will be unable to mirror. In other words, the more you cater to each customer, the less interested they will be in competitors who are unable to achieve the same level of individual attention, simply because they don't have access to the same customer information. Each customer, by virtue of her or his relationship with you, invests in your company by providing you with information about how best to please him or her. The greater their investment, the less inclined they will be to do business elsewhere. The ultimate result is win-win, a truly mutually beneficial relationship between client and company."

Elaine thanked the participant and applauded her. Nearly everyone followed suit, having transitioned quickly from spectators to active participants. Elaine held out a valuable state lottery ticket.

"Let me elaborate a bit on convenience, a critical customer benefit. Who doesn't appreciate convenience? Who doesn't get perturbed when they must wait in long lines, or repeat the same information to a clerk over and over? To successfully cultivate relationships, companies must design systems and implement service procedures that contribute to increasing the customer's pleasure in doing business so the result is win-win.

"Here's an example you'll like. Some auto manufacturers are currently installing a system called OnStar in some of their cars. OnStar's technology is an interactive information exchange between your 'smart car' and OnStar representatives in various locations around the U.S. and Canada. Actually, the system integrates cellular technology with the GPS system, which allows the OnStar service center to not only know the exact location of your vehicle at any given time but also to provide the ultimate in convenience. OnStar says it is the world's most comprehensive in-vehicle safety, security, and communication service, so let's see the kind of *intimacy* you have when you drive a Chevrolet, Buick, GMC, SAAB, or other OnStar-equipped vehicles.

"Let's say you lock your keys in the car. Who hasn't made this mistake? Well, as an OnStar customer, you can call the service center, and using your personal secret code, notify the OnStar rep to 'send' an electronic signal to activate your vehicle's electronic locking system. You are able to get back on the road within seconds. In terms of convenience, that's the ultimate! But that's not all. If you 'lose' your car in a large parking lot, OnStar can activate your car's horn by remote control, so it can 'call' to you!

"With convenience like that, you will never again feel like you're driving alone," she concluded and decided to read the next component herself.

6: ADVANTAGES

Over time, as the customer comes to enjoy the developing relationship, she will eventually expect the advantages and perks that distinguish your company from others. Every time you meet or exceed the customer's expectations, she or he is reminded that you bring a certain added value that continually strengthens the intimate relationship.

Steve Jobs has demonstrated that concept throughout the last thirty years. Apple brought us new products and solutions that gave us absolute advantages, while changing our habits.

iPod, iPhone, iPad, iTunes are a few of those products that changed the world. But Steve jobs knows also that, as customers are tempted by competitors' increasingly sophisticated efforts to attract new business, they will still expect you to reward their loyalty with exemplary service and extra benefits, for which they, in turn, will remain faithful partners.

Elaine paused and asked the group if they could think of specific examples of absolute advantages that smart companies extend to their most loyal customers. A few of the examples they shared were these:

1. The airline that enables its best customers to book a flight at the last minute.
2. The retail shop that opens the store after hours just for a certain group of customers.
3. The store that notifies its best customers of a clearance sale, a few weeks before the sale is made public.
4. The company that doubles its warranty free of charge for their most loyal customers.

Suddenly, an unidentified red-headed man wearing a Calvin Klein suit raised his hand and said, "Every customer should also feel that there is added value on an emotional level. There should be some kind of emotional hook that makes customers become company champions, to become the kind of people who will sing the company's praises in every situation, from an informal conversation to recommending services to family, friends, or associates."

Elaine thanked him, commenting, "Wow! I have a partner to tango with here, and I have a present for you!" She walked over to her podium and retrieved a box wrapped in tissue paper. The entire group was curious about its contents, including Daniel. Elaine then asked the man to open the box. He did as he was asked and, inside, found Usher's best-selling *Confessions* CD. Daniel was rooted to his chair.

Elaine decided to share another true story. "Five hundred years ago, well not so long ago, although sometimes it feels like that...Michael Dell, president of Dell Computers, succeeded in marketing the PC and grabbed a sizeable share of the global market as a result of developing and implementing an Intimate Marketing culture. Naturally, he didn't invite every woman who bought one of his computers to a restaurant for a cozy candlelight dinner. But everyone who bought a Dell PC from him was invited to call a special service center twenty-four hours a day, seven days a week, to obtain assistance with any kind of PC problem imaginable. Customers, recognizing that, sooner or later, they might need that kind of assistance, appreciated the offer and bought from Dell. That was his key selling proposition. He created a relative advantage over his competitors and took an enormous chunk out of the market.

"It goes without saying that customers, while conversing with representatives from the Dell hotline, provide a wealth of information about their needs and Dell's ability to meet those needs. This gives the company an opportunity to sell additional software and services— an example of Intimate Marketing at its best. Now, who's volunteering to read the next point?"

Daniel Marks was preparing to raise his hand, but Mister Calvin Klein grabbed the chance and started to read!

7: TAILORED TREATMENT

As part of the intimate connection system, the other party expects you to respond quickly to his/her needs. As you know, we all measure the depth of our friendships when times are tough, and the saying, "a friend in need is a friend indeed," becomes very relevant. Complaints are great opportunities to prove that you are not just a "fair-weather friend," but rather that you are there when customers need you most, ready and able to listen and respond to their individual concerns.

Elaine Sherman returned to the platform. "In creating an Intimate Marketing culture, the company must ensure that all customer demands are answered quickly and effectively, no matter how unusual." Here, she took another breath and announced that she wanted to relate a personal experience to everyone.

"About two weeks ago, I phoned International Airlines, where I am a member of the Frequent Flyer program, and made a request that was a little bit out of the ordinary. A friend of mine was booked on an IA flight on his birthday..."

Daniel Marks felt himself redden, slowly but surely. This time, he was not mistaken. He was certain that the steadfast gaze of Ms. Intimate Marketing was focused directly on him. For a moment, he hoped no one would notice her staring at him. But after the initial panic, he regained his composure by thinking about his distinguished position, his achievements, and his winning personality. Suddenly, he no longer felt afraid of Elaine Sherman's gaze or rebuke. If and when the opportunity presented itself, he would be happy to enrich her with *his* knowledge of business management and marketing. *I didn't receive my MBA cum laude from Harvard University for anything*, he reminded himself.

Elaine was continuing with her story. "I very much wanted my friend to be surprised by a very special gift from me, and a happy birthday greeting delivered by an attendant during the long flight. My request certainly didn't cost much. But what was their response? One guess: they simply could not grant my request. It was impossible.

"A company managing a preferred customers club, especially a prestigious company like International Airlines, should have jumped at the opportunity to meet my needs. Especially when it meant granting an extraordinary request. This was their chance to really 'wow' me with the special treatment that I, and other members of an 'exclusive' program, expect. This philosophy forms the basic premise of Intimate Marketing, and keeps customers loyal, even in the face of 'special deals' from the competition. Think about it: when service from one company is just like that of the competition, why stay faithful? Without intimacy, there will be no loyalty. Only when a customer is receiving superb care is the idea of 'betrayal' out of the question."

For a moment, Daniel hoped the ground would open up and swallow him whole.

"Could you please give us some examples of smart intimate treatment?" asked one of the participants.

"Sure. Let's go back to OnStar. It's obvious that one of the customer benefits is OnStar's ability to locate stolen vehicles. In and of itself, that service is not unique to OnStar. But here's the added value that turned this potentially 'ordinary' company into one with an exemplary reputation. First, their service hotline is available twenty-four hours a day to provide travel directions for customers. Requests are virtually limitless: customers can ask for detailed directions to a particular address or the location of the nearest gas station, cash station, or McDonald's. If remembering the verbal directions is problematic, OnStar's system allows customers to record the instructions and replay them as many times as necessary.

"While all these services are nice, it's possible to live without them. However, in my opinion, the most important service they provide is the automatic rescue system. Listen to this—up to the minute emergency care! Let's say, for example, that your car is involved in a traffic accident. The moment your front airbag inflates,

OnStar staff will see it in their computers! They make immediate contact with you to find out if help is needed, and if you don't answer right away, they will dial nine-one-one and report your exact location. We're talking about something *beyond* care–this is a special treatment that can actually save lives.

"That's a relative advantage par excellence with this company, and it brings us to the next point on the handouts."

Elaine proceeded to the eighth and final point on the pastel page and read:

8: ENTREPRENEURSHIP

"Innovate or die," said management guru Tom Peters. Customers today expect your company to 'go the extra mile' in terms of customer relations and customer service. Like most of us, they expect to be surprised by the introduction of new concepts, products, and services. Just as romantic partners work to introduce variety into their personal lives, so must the company introduce innovative options to its customers, which is part of Intimate Marketing. Customers demand services above and beyond the previously respectable high level of quality. Today, companies must keep customers' adrenaline flowing by amazing them over and over again. The ability to keep things fresh and new comes from fostering creativity and taking initiative—two key traits of true entrepreneurs.

The best way to achieve freshness and variety is to think like an entrepreneur. That means working to break new ground, seeing things from new perspectives, and daring to be different.

People who think like an entrepreneur give 200 percent. Understanding that everything they do reflects back on them and influences results, they tend to take their work seriously. In addition, they often struggle to develop and sustain flexibility and adaptability to keep pace with the customer's ever-changing demands and needs.

At a time when competition is stiff, a time when it has become increasingly more difficult to 'wow' the customer, creative thinking and daring must take the initiative to do the unexpected, both of which are traits of an entrepreneur and can make all the difference."

Elaine asked the whole group to discuss at their tables the eight parts of Intimate Marketing and share their thoughts about the concept for exactly twenty-four minutes. People enjoyed participating in the process and they liked to hear some new ideas about how to apply the Intimate Marketing principles.

"Let me give you one more tip before we take a twenty-minute break," Elaine said.

"We all live in Mark Zuckerberg's Facebook world and we all play a part in the connected society. But the opposite of 'network' is…'not-work' and we should always create intimate relations in the old-school way, face-to-face, and not only with the new media school. The fact that you have five thousand online friends does not imply that you have one true intimate soul mate. So, use the break to connect, to interact, to network, and to add value to each other. I will see you all in twenty intimate minutes."

* * *

Some of the participants immediately rose from their chairs and headed for the refreshment table. Daniel Marks remained seated. He really, truly, dreaded the direct encounter that awaited him with the nervy woman who wrote him the pale purple letter. He listed the headings of the discussion points one under another, and was not really surprised at the result: I-N-T-I-M-A-T-E. *I wonder if this sharp lady knows what real intimacy is*, he thought. By now, he was more determined than ever to check her out up close.

He got up from his seat, but stopped suddenly in his tracks. There was Elaine Sherman, casually standing next to the refreshment table carrying on light conversation with several people. She didn't look deeply engrossed in the discussion, as if the person who really interested and excited her was not among those gathered around her. *But what will I say to her? Just introduce myself and shake her hand? Maybe she won't even remember me. Maybe I need to be original and creative, do something really different at this crucial, initial meeting.*

Lost in thought, Daniel remained standing, somewhat hesitant. Suddenly, Elaine excused herself from the conversations at the refreshment table and walked toward him.

"Hi, Daniel," she said and extended her hand. Daniel gave her one of his most heartfelt smiles and returned the gesture. "I'm really glad you didn't forget about my seminar and that you were able to make it," she said with simple sincerity. Daniel was mentally thanking her for sparing him the embarrassed response that he had been prepared to share.

"I'm enjoying your presentation very much," he said, expecting her to pursue the subject further so that he could immerse himself in her deep blue eyes. He wanted to hear more about her consulting firm and about how she applied the theories to her own clients. But more than anything, he wanted to know whether or not she had a man waiting for her at home. He was sure that a woman this pleasant and successful would not be spending much time alone. Unfortunately, while he was musing about these possibilities, the coffee break ended, and everyone returned to their seats. Elaine thanked Daniel for the compliment, excused herself, and a moment later, resumed her role as charismatic and intriguing speaker.

"Is there one component among the eight you think is most important?" Elaine asked. "Right, they are all equally important. All of them jointly create the correct combination for maximum results. That's synergy. The heart of Intimate Marketing is your database. But before I explain this topic, try to imagine what it was like for me more than twenty years ago when I was growing up in Albany, New York.

"I lived with my family in a small neighborhood. Down the street was a little grocery store. To this day, I can still remember that the store manager always knew just what produce and cuts of meat my mother wanted in preparation for the weekend, and even in what quantities. When my mom and I would enter his store, he would say, 'Hi there, Mrs. Sherman, shall I wrap up *the usual* for you?' My mom would smile and nod, and within minutes, the meat and produce would be weighed, wrapped, and prepared. At the nearby ice cream parlor, I received similar treatment: the woman at the counter knew that when I asked for my 'usual' cone, I meant the same two scoops of a certain chocolate combination I always bought.

"This was Intimate Marketing at its finest, even though we're talking about an era before YouTube, Google, or cell phones in kindergartens...Alfredo the grocer and Pauline the ice cream lady did everything they could to keep us happy. Giving us personal attention and service came naturally to them. They remembered all their customers' names, always wished us well on all the holidays, and during the busiest times, extended their business hours to accommodate people's busy schedules. If someone from our family failed to show up for a few weeks, they worried and inquired about our welfare.

"Intimate Marketing applies the same principles used in the past, just on a larger scale. Computerization helps us to remember much more information about many more customers. Let's see..."

Before Elaine could finish her sentence, the hall was suddenly plunged into complete darkness. After a confusing minute or so, participants began lighting matches, or turned their smart phones into flashlights, using whatever they had available. A maintenance man from the Marriott entered the room and announced that a major power source had blown, and it would be some time before it would be remedied. Elaine regained her composure quickly and turned the problem into an opportunity. "There's no better way to end the first session on Intimate Marketing than with an intimate atmosphere of darkness. The hotel will undoubtedly compensate us at our next meeting," she added pointedly. "Now, please start to plan effective ways to apply the eight principles of Intimate Marketing for your business. I will see you next week!"

Slowly, the participants filed through the exit. From a distance, random flashlights flickered, illuminating the way for those heading through the main exit. Daniel was among those making his way toward the door, wondering how he would locate his vehicle in the blacked-out underground parking lot.

"Come on, we'll look for our cars together," he heard Elaine's voice close by. "The truth is I'm not crazy about entering a dark parking lot alone."

Daniel smiled to himself with satisfaction. At last, a small weak spot in Elaine Sherman's armor. Soon he would learn how to take advantage of that.

They descended to the parking lot, measuring their steps with care. Suddenly, Elaine tripped and let out a choked cry. Daniel hurried to grab her and set her back on her feet. Elaine instinctively grabbed the hand he held out for support. He hoped she wouldn't be quick to let it go and wasn't disappointed. Elaine continued to hold his hand under the pretense of simply keeping each other steady, as they made their way to their cars. Daniel was thankful for the darkness, because it kept her from seeing the sudden blush on his face.

The underground parking lot seemed much less threatening than they had imagined. One by one, car owners found their vehicles and switched on their headlights, providing some dim light. "My car is parked over there, on the left," said Elaine, obviously expecting Daniel to accompany her to the door. "There, that's mine." She pointed to a brand-new silver Alfa Romeo 8C Spider. She got in and turned the ignition, but the car wouldn't start. Daniel volunteered his help, trying different key-turning strategies, but had no better luck.

"I'm sure the parking manager will keep an eye on your Alfa. Meanwhile, let's find my car and I'll drive you home." Daniel sounded decisive and firm. Elaine liked that. They continued walking close together in the darkness until they reached Daniel's four-by-four, with the International Airlines sticker on his front windshield. Daniel opened the passenger door, and Elaine settled comfortably into the soft seat.

She asked him to drive her home and gave him the address of a newly renovated block of Old Town New York. Daniel shifted gears and they drove off. At first, a brief but awkward silence surrounded them. "So…how did you learn so much about marketing?" Daniel asked her.

"First of all, I have a lot of life experience. I've also read many books on the subject." Her answer surprised Daniel. He had expected her to drop names of prestigious universities and a list of degrees ending *cum laude*, the snobbish label of excellence. It soon became clear that Elaine did have degrees, but in psychology and computer science. "I set out to learn what I didn't know but wanted to know," she explained. She also mentioned that, in her spare time, she enjoyed playing the piano, especially jazz, and she devoured adventure novels.

When they reached her home, a mellow brownstone on a quiet, tree-lined street, Daniel regretted that their meeting was ending so soon, so he mustered the courage to ask, "What do you say about getting together for dinner tomorrow evening?"

Elaine smiled and replied, "I'd really love to. I'm sure I'll be able to get my car started by then. I probably just forgot to cancel something. That's what happens when you buy a car with a computerized system more complex than a spaceship. Where do you live? I'll be happy to pick you up."

The idea appealed to Daniel. They agreed to talk by phone at seven o'clock the next evening. For several long minutes, he stared at her retreating figure, as she passed through the doorway, turned on the light, and ascended the stairs. He waited until the second floor lights lit up and then directed his attention to his surroundings and drove home to his small studio apartment on 58th street where his beloved cat, Tiger, was waiting for him as usual.

Chapter 3

The Rendezvous

As Elaine entered her apartment, she kicked off her shoes, pulled off her clothing, and headed straight for the shower. Although she didn't think much of Daniel Marks' professionalism as manager of the Frequent Flyer program, there was something about him that definitely attracted her. Was it his commanding presence? Or maybe his heartfelt smile? Or was it just that she was proud of how easily she had drawn him into her orbit?

The water washed over her body. After a brisk toweling and massage with some body lotion given to her by her last boyfriend, she collected some magazines she hadn't yet had time to read and tossed them onto her bed. Still undressed, she slipped under the comforter and settled in for the night.

* * *

The next day, Daniel arrived at work early because he knew he would have to leave in time to go home, to freshen up, and to prepare for his date with Elaine. He also felt he should review the information about his Frequent Flyer program customers and think about how he could apply the Intimate Marketing theory. He knew he owed Elaine a thank you for urging him to attend her seminar.

* * *

When Elaine reached her office at around ten that morning, the first thing she did was call her friend Norma, a systems analyst at International Airlines. Norma, when asked what she knew about Daniel Marks, replied, "You don't stand a chance. He's a hot item, and what's more, he knows it. All the single girls at IA are trying to catch his eye, but he doesn't even give them a second glance. It is common knowledge that he is single, but no one knows if he's seeing anyone."

"We're going out tonight," Elaine announced.

There was silence on Norma's end of the phone. "Good luck," she finally said. "I'm dying to hear what happens."

* * *

Precisely at seven that evening, Elaine's cell phone rang. It was Daniel. In a friendly, casual tone, he successfully masked the excitement in his voice. Elaine tried to maintain a relaxed and pleasant voice, as well. They agreed she would pick him up from his place on 58th street at nine o'clock. "You *have* to meet Tiger," Daniel teased. Elaine agreed to go to his apartment.

A moment before knocking on his door, Elaine felt a twinge of self-consciousness, but there was no way out now. Daniel opened the door, and she caught the scent of expensive after-shave. The apartment was small but pleasant; it looked as if Daniel had given a lot of thought to the decor. Tiger, his gray cat, purred contentedly when he saw Elaine. *A good sign,* Daniel thought. *Tiger doesn't often warm up to people easily.*

Daniel offered Elaine some coffee and chocolate chip cookies. "You have to try this coffee—I brought it from Milan." Elaine accepted it willingly. She didn't know exactly what they were going to discuss throughout the evening; she only hoped they wouldn't discuss Intimate Marketing. She felt they had already exhausted that subject. Surely there were many other things to talk about with Daniel Marks, and if not, then she would find a way to end the meeting quickly and excuse herself.

Daniel came back carrying a tray with two cups of espresso, exuding an unfamiliar aroma. He was in no hurry to leave the house for their planned evening out. Like her, he felt very comfortable and didn't want to cut it short too soon. Also like Elaine, he hoped that they wouldn't discuss the details of Intimate Marketing. True, the theory appealed to him, so much so that he had decided to apply its principles at IA as soon as he could. But at this moment, Daniel was hoping for a different kind of intimacy, much closer, and much more personal.

For two full minutes they enjoyed the Italian coffee in total silence. Elaine's eyes traveled around the room, drinking in its tasteful decor. Daniel, meanwhile, was concentrating on her. From time to time he dared to steal a look at her blue eyes.

"In a week, I'm going to a Harvard alumni reunion," he said suddenly. Elaine smiled and waited for him to continue with some anecdotes from his academic past or his fraternity adventures. For some reason, she thought men always wanted to open a conversation with some macho story about their university experiences.

Suddenly, Elaine's cell phone rang. She answered reluctantly, and immediately her face clouded. "I'll be there right away," she answered. "My father was just admitted to the hospital and they don't know what's wrong with him," she said to Daniel.

"Do you want me to go with you?" he asked sympathetically.

"No, but thank you for offering," Elaine said with a distant and preoccupied tone. "If you could see me to the door though..." They descended the stairs in silence. Elaine slipped into her Alfa and suddenly remembered something. "I almost forgot. I brought you a little gift. Here, take this and look it over when you have a few minutes." She started the car. "Thanks for the coffee. I must go now. Ciao!" She sped off into the darkness.

Daniel Marks took the large envelope in both hands and stared at it for a few moments before opening it. The words, *Intimate Marketing: What Is It?* were written on the pale violet cover. He felt a tinge of disappointment as he turned to go back upstairs. Tiger playfully attacked him as he entered the apartment. Having nothing else planned for the evening, he decided to retire early and read. He took off his clothes, curled up under the covers, turned on the small reading lamp, and began to read the booklet Elaine had given him—the most tangible reminder he had of her at that moment. *How romantic.*

Some of the sections were already familiar to him, so he skipped over them quickly. *Let's define Intimate Marketing,* were the words dancing before his eyes.

Intimate Marketing is a computerized system used to gather relevant information about a company's existing and potential customers. Its purpose is to enable the company to provide customers with such superb service that their expectations are exceeded, and to establish friendly, long-term relationships, from which both parties profit.

Research shows that successful marketing of this type raises customer loyalty, reduces marketing expenditures, and increases customer satisfaction, bottom line sales, and profits.

The database allows marketers to target offers to existing and potential customers. This will ensure that each customer receives the most appropriate offer at the right time and under the right terms. Targeted efforts like this will increase customer response from all avenues of contact.

Using data effectively generally increases customer response rates relative to marketing costs. Direct sales expenditures decrease and company profits increase.

The more skilled a company is at using information to understand the customer's perspective, the better it will be at meeting customer needs. The customer feels understood and therefore also understands (maybe even subconsciously) and appreciates the concept of Intimate Marketing. Moreover, the customer experiences the relative advantages of belonging to an exclusive group—a group that receives preferential treatment from the company.

So, if the idea of Intimate Marketing is so great, why do so few companies apply its principles?

Why, indeed? Daniel asked himself and decided to read another chapter before his eyes closed and he drifted off to sleep.

I'll give you eight reasons, wrote Elaine, and Daniel felt as if she had written the words especially for him.

1. Lack of proper design

Most of the customer programs or clubs established in recent years simply were not designed properly. They were developed primarily from the company's perspective, often just one of many marketing efforts.

Most companies don't understand that with effective marketing (what we call 'intimate') the customer must be the focus that drives the whole process. Every element is designed, developed, and revised in response to constantly changing customer profiles.

2. A 'customer club' without substance

Most companies introduce a customer club much like a fitness center. Typically, you are entitled to participate in the various sports activities for one annual fee.

Management doesn't realize you come in every Monday morning at 5:30 and leave after an hour. They don't know that your spouse visits the fitness room two afternoons per week, and that you both play bridge there every Tuesday evening. Since there is no dialogue, and they fail to capture usage data about your family, they have no practical means for identifying new services based upon client preferences.

A fitness center that operates a customer club as described above is missing an enormous opportunity—a common mistake of many companies. Without dialogue or some other way to build a mutually satisfying relationship between the fitness center and the customer, such clubs will soon fail. Those who are successful constantly measure and evaluate customer satisfaction, taking care to address each perceived weakness. Management must be realistic in its assessment of strengths and weaknesses, using feedback to determine which activities warrant greater investment and which should be eliminated or scaled back.

3. Failure to define specific and relevant goals

Intimate Marketing must form the basis of the overall marketing plan. Without a marketing plan or program, there is no point in initiating an Intimate Marketing culture. After all, if you don't know where you are going, how will you know when you arrive?

That is exactly what happens with many companies. They establish a customer club because it is trendy, just as manufacturers copy successful products. If a credit card company distributes a 'Gold' membership, its competitors follow with a 'Gold' card too or a 'Platinum' card. Copycat marketing has nothing in common with the one-on-one appeal of Intimate Marketing.

Therefore, the key to success with Intimate Marketing is to define realistic, achievable, and measurable goals. The more focused you are during this phase, the more likely you are to achieve your goals using Intimate Marketing as an effective tool. Smart goals will meet the five criteria listed below:

- **Specific**—Goals should be defined in specific terms. General goals lack the necessary focus. Everyone in the company must understand each goal so that there is no doubt about the company's direction.
- **Measurable**—Each goal must be defined in a way that makes it possible to measure the company's progress.
- **Attainable**—There is no point in setting an unattainable goal. It's okay to think big, but it's better to begin with a small, challenging but

reasonable goal. If the goal is too lofty, failure can dampen enthusiasm and reduce your credibility with customers (and employees).

- **Realistic**—The goal must be within the scope of marketing reality. While it's true that realism can be subjective, it is fair to say that a goal of 100 percent customer retention is unlikely for reasons beyond anyone's control, as is trying to achieve a growth rate of 500 percent within a limited time period. Remember that disappointment is a function of expectations.
- **Timely**—You must set a schedule for achieving your goals. The more detailed the schedule, the greater the likelihood of staying on task and making steady progress. A goal without a deadline is only a dream.

To summarize, before you design an Intimate Marketing culture, commit your goals to paper, with as much detail as possible. Thoroughly define exactly what you want to achieve, when you want to have achieved it, what resources you will commit, and who will be committed to implementing each step.

Daniel liked the five criteria for smart goals. He noticed that the first initials of each point created the word SMART. *A really smart idea*, he thought, as the booklet began slipping out of his hands. A quick look at his 44 mm yellow gold YachtMaster Rolex reminded him it was getting late. His eyes had managed to close more than once in the last hour. Goals? Schedules? In those moments when he closed his eyes, he imagined Elaine sitting next to him on the bed, reading aloud the sections she had written. He heard her voice, as if she were reading a love letter to him. Even in his state of semi-consciousness he thought, *my goal is to make Elaine mine...When? As soon as possible...I hope.*

As far as strategy went, he would have to think that through in the morning when his mind was clearer. Maybe on his way to work he could select an appropriate strategy. *Tomorrow*, he promised himself, *I'll continue reading Elaine's booklet.* Despite it being a professional business booklet, Daniel felt especially close to Elaine, just knowing she wrote the words. It even carried her scent. He held it close to him as he drifted off to sleep—with a smile on his face.

Morning came much too quickly. The alarm clock rang, and Daniel reluctantly opened his eyes to begin his hectic day. The remnants of a sweet dream hung on, a dream in which he and Elaine were racing across a quiet, unspoiled desert in a red jeep. He woke up, just as he was dreaming of pouring a tall glass of cold sparkling champagne for her.

At eight o'clock, after finishing his espresso, he grabbed his iPad and headed out the door to work. The stairwell was quiet. Suddenly, he recalled Elaine's shocked face the previous evening when she learned the news about her father. *I must call her and ask how she's doing, and how her father is doing*, he thought. *I'll wait until ten o'clock or so to place the call.*

Walking down the hallway on the way to his office, he met Norma Allen, the tall, slender systems analyst. She greeted him with a conspiratorial smile and an overly emphatic "Good morning, Daniel." Daniel returned her greeting, still unaware of the relationship between Norma, the computer lady he'd never really noticed before, and Elaine, the newly discovered object of his dreams.

At two minutes past ten, he called Elaine. Although longing to hear her voice, more important to him was hearing good news about her father's condition. Elaine answered on the third ring. "I was hoping it would be you," she said. "My father is out of danger. He's already been moved from intensive care. By the way, I told him about you."

"About me?" Daniel repeated in amazement.

"Yes, I told him that his timing was really awful, that the call about his hospitalization came while I was out on a date with a nice man, who needed marketing expertise. I think that's when I saw him smile for the first time!"

"I'm glad I was able to make him smile," said Daniel. "And more importantly, I'm glad things worked out well. Give him my wishes for a speedy recovery. And as far as I'm concerned, we can resume our meeting tonight where we left off."

"I'm not sure I want to be away from the hospital," Elaine replied. "But maybe you could drop by here after work. We can sit in the hospital cafeteria. By the way, did you have any time to read the booklet I gave you?"

Daniel told her that he had read as far as the chapter on SMART goals. "Great," she said. "Maybe you can bring the booklet with you and we can continue discussing Intimate Marketing."

Daniel swallowed. This was not exactly what he had in mind. There were so many other things he wanted to know about her, but he decided to go along with the game. "Sure, I'll bring it," he promised and decided it could be useful to him if the conversation lagged. After all, he still barely knew her, and, given the situation, anything could happen.

* * *

Daniel counted the minutes until seven o'clock. He arrived at the hospital after a quick stop at home to shower, change clothes, and pick up Elaine's booklet. He called Elaine from the parking lot, and she informed him that his cup of coffee was waiting for him.

He entered the cafeteria hesitantly. At first glance, it didn't feel like the right setting for this meeting, but when he caught sight of Elaine's captivating shape, the environment seemed unimportant. He approached her, kissing her lightly on the cheek. For a moment there was silence. "You'll have to thank my father for releasing me for this meeting," she said, smiling. He looked into her eyes and noted with relief that the worry he had seen yesterday was gone.

Looking down at the table, he spotted a plate of chocolate chip cookies next to his coffee. "I ordered them especially for you," she said, and Daniel was pleased. "Daniel, I like you very much. I am so glad I was angry at IA and wrote you the letter. You see, in my world of Intimate Marketing, a complaint is a gift. Now, with your permission," she said suddenly, "I would like to discuss why so few businesses apply the Intimate Marketing culture, or do try it but fail."

Daniel felt a strange thrill travel through his spine. Only yesterday he had dreamed about a private lesson like this. "How far did you say you got in your reading?" Elaine brought his attention back with the question.

Daniel opened the booklet and leafed through it. "The fourth reason," he answered.

4. Failure to plan

Once you've completed the goal-setting stage, you must be careful to avoid a common mistake: neglecting to prepare a detailed plan. This is the only way to transform long-term goals into a series of smaller, achievable steps, all of which must meet the five 'SMART' criteria we examined earlier:

You must first define the specific steps, and then list them in the appropriate order. The order is extremely important. Just as there are well-defined steps for building a house (foundation, frame, brickwork, plastering, etc.), so must there be a practical sequence for business planning. When creating your plan, try to avoid formulating it from your own viewpoint. You must view it from the customer's perspective as well as that of the company.

5. Building with the 'wham-bam' method

The 'wham-bam' philosophy sacrifices thoughtful planning in the interest of saving time. Understandably, many companies get excited, and rightfully so, about the idea of establishing a customer club. However, in their enthusiasm, they dive in without adequate preparation. Just as a one-night stand between a man and a woman rarely results in long-term romance, a few days of haphazard planning is never enough to establish the foundation for a long-term, intimate, customer relationship. Like the one-night stand, once the hasty plan is complete, you'll find yourself wondering "what next?" Many companies fail at instituting successful customer clubs because they employ the 'wham-bam' approach.

6. Building at a snail's pace

This is the antithesis of the preceding point. One common mistake in building an Intimate Marketing culture is progressing too slowly. If you decide to implement it three years from now, don't be surprised to find yourself lagging way behind your competitors. In three years, you will have lost your customers' loyalty. To attract and keep them, you must take action now. Today, there are two kinds of organizations in the world: the quick-moving ones and the dead ones.

Company size is no justification for delaying the implementation of Intimate Marketing principles. Just as a man cannot develop intimate relations with all the women in New York City, a large company must choose the most appropriate customers with whom to begin. By the way, it is not necessary to start with the most important group. You can start with any group at all. The goal is to learn from your mistakes, correct them, and then apply the program to your most valuable customers, and eventually all customers.

7. Failure to ask the key question

Most of the companies that fail in establishing good customer relationships make one small, but critical, mistake. They forget to ask a key question: "What are the benefits to our customers?" or "Why would our customers want to be members of this 'club?'"

Don't be myopic in your perspective. Think about the customer first. The best way to form a club is in cooperation with your customers. Focus groups or even informal customer research can help you identify which features to offer. When you begin developing a relationship, find out what speaks to your customers. Test several ideas with a small group first— ask them which services they feel add the most value, and consider their opinions when making decisions concerning which features to offer.

8. Falling into the 'Catch-22' trap

Budgetary constraints stop many companies in their tracks. Let's say you are a marketing manager for a baby-care products company. You attend a managers' meeting to present the idea of implementing an Intimate Marketing culture. Everyone looks at you in amazement, and the jokes begin to roll: "What kind of intimacy did you have in mind?"

Eventually, the room settles down, you present your idea, and it sounds promising—except for one thing: you have no proof that it will work. This is the 'Catch-22.' You want budget approval, but without a successful track record, how can you expect to get it? And yet, without a reasonable budget, you won't even be able to start.

Daniel glanced over at Elaine's face, noticing how serious she had suddenly become. She didn't look up at him, as she was totally focused on her booklet. He tried hard to pay close attention to the phrases as she read, but occasionally, he would catch himself watching her with much more interest than he felt for the marketing theories she was reading.

A well-groomed woman in her sixties approached them. "I'm Rochelle, Elaine's mother. It's nice to meet you," she introduced herself to Daniel. "Dad is feeling much better, and he would like to see you now," she said to Elaine.

Elaine turned her gaze to Daniel, who froze in his seat for a moment. Would it be proper for him to accompany Elaine to visit her father? Would it embarrass her? Or him? He hoped Elaine would help him with his decision.

"Will you come with me?" she asked in an easy, natural way, and Daniel smiled at her with relief.

"Of course," he answered.

The two of them left the cafeteria and approached the elevators. Elaine pushed the button for the third floor. Her face once more grew serious. Daniel disliked the hospital smell and the sterile, omnipresent whiteness. It seemed to him that Elaine too wished she could put on colored glasses to brighten the drab surroundings.

The room where David, Elaine's father, was hospitalized was quiet and cool. Metal tubes ran in all directions, and it took Daniel a few minutes to become accustomed to the surroundings. David smiled at him and gave him a strong handshake. "Elaine told me about you," he said. "But only good things," he added, and gave Daniel a quick man-to-man wink.

Daniel didn't know exactly what to say. He remembered an uncle of his who underwent a catheterization two years before and had learned then that it wasn't wise to discuss medical problems—better to be optimistic. Apparently, David Sherman perceived Daniel's dilemma and initiated a conversation.

"So, where are the preferred destinations these days on International Airlines?" he asked. "After I'm finished here with all this recovery business, I'm taking Rochelle and flying somewhere exotic where we can live it up and have a good time."

Daniel felt a little embarrassed. It was true that he was the manager of the Frequent Flyer program, but he had never been asked questions like these, and he simply didn't know the answer. "I'll check on that for you, and tomorrow I'll give you a detailed answer," he promised and made a mental note to do so, first thing in the morning.

"Like Elaine, I'm also a member of your Frequent Flyer program. And I have to say, we have noticed the difference since your management changed," David continued, and Daniel felt uncomfortable. He was actually able to remember thousands of club members by name, but after meeting Elaine, he really should have thought to check if any other family members were on the preferred customers list.

Elaine kissed her father on the forehead and promised to visit him tomorrow. Daniel said that he would come, too, bringing the promised destination list. He was secretly happy about taking this initiative, because it gave him an excuse to spend yet another day in the company of the beautiful young woman at his side.

Together, they made their way across the crowded parking lot in silence. Surprisingly, they discovered that their cars were parked side by side. *Funny I didn't notice it before*, Daniel thought, but he saw it as a good omen. For a moment, it seemed that Elaine was in no rush to leave, as if she didn't want this meeting to end. But suddenly her car started and off she drove, shouting a warm goodbye out the window, saying that she would see him again tomorrow, same time, and same place.

Daniel had wanted to hold her, to feel her by his side, if only for a brief moment. But Elaine was flying off into the night in her shiny new car, leaving him alone on an evening with such romantic potential. He climbed into his four-by-four, and drove toward his small, but homey, apartment.

* * *

Elaine was driving while listening to her favorite album, "Mack the Knife: The Complete Ella in Berlin," which she had downloaded in MP3 format.

Although she was light-years away from the Ella Fitzgerald era, she felt a connection with her favorite jazz singer. Elaine Sherman had it all: money; a good family; a comfortable, sheltered life; and people who appreciated and even admired her. But she wanted love, too, the real love of a man for a woman, a love that would pierce her to her depths, through the many layers and facets of her strong personality.

She wanted to come home at night to a warm home and a man who really loved her, who knew how to listen, to hold and support her, who would be her best friend, as well as an exciting lover. *Could Daniel be the one?* she asked herself. To her surprise, she didn't reject the possibility outright. Daniel Marks was certainly an attractive man, eyed by many women. But she felt that, in spite of his academic prowess, he still had a lot to learn about what life had to offer. *If he would only agree, and not feel threatened, I would be happy to share my knowledge and experience with him*, she thought.

Maybe I have to let go a little, give him a break, and not be so forceful. Suddenly she felt uneasy. "This always happens to me," she said aloud to the crooning Ella. "Why do I have to prove to everyone how smart I am?" *If Daniel hasn't given up on me yet, I'll try from now on to give him the lead, and see where he can take this relationship.*

The car glided into its parking space. Elaine climbed the white steps and opened the door of her tastefully decorated apartment. Then, for the first time in her life, she closed her eyes and imagined she would open them to find Daniel standing there in front of her, smiling. It was clear to her that she felt something for him. But she didn't yet dare to assume the feelings were mutual.

At ten o'clock the next morning, Elaine called her father, but there was no answer. Filled with fear, she dialed her mother's cell-phone number. "Don't worry, dad is fine. They're examining him, and in a little while they're going to release him." Elaine's heart was filled with joy. Only now could she admit to herself how worried she had been. More than once the thought had occurred to her, what would happen if she were to lose him now?

It was true that, in the past, there had been more than a little friction between them. Once, they even had a loud confrontation, when at the age of sixteen she had brought home a new boyfriend ten years her senior. But she knew that, deep down, her father loved her very much, and she loved him too. She also was indebted to him for the unwavering support he had provided for as long as she could remember. Not every father encouraged his ambitious daughter to develop her own business with as much love and enthusiasm as he had, especially in such a competitive field. Not every father, who himself worked as a salaried employee, would be genuinely pleased with his daughter's courage to open a business at age twenty-six. She had to say, however, she had done really well for herself in only six years of running her own business.

Her first impulse at that moment was to call Daniel and tell him the good news. For a second, the thought occurred to her that maybe it was too early to reveal her vulnerability. But on second thought, he deserved to know, since only yesterday he had been visiting her father, too, and had left the hospital looking worried.

"I'm really happy for you and for your parents," Daniel said to Elaine on the phone. "We have to celebrate. I'd like to take you to a place very different from where we met yesterday," he announced.

Elaine was ready. "Where are you thinking about taking me?"

"My secret," Daniel replied with confidence. "Just do me a favor, don't come with your cell-phone turned on and dressed in a business suit. By the way, I'll be at your house tonight at seven. Bye."

He hung up abruptly, surprised at his own boldness. He had no idea where he was going to take Elaine that evening, but clearly it had to be far, far away from the hospital. He had an important meeting in five minutes with his CEO, but he simply could not concentrate on his work. His brain was racing non-stop, until suddenly, he found a solution that laid his mind to rest.

Chapter 4

Business before Pleasure

Elaine had to admit she was pretty excited about the surprise awaiting her. She had no idea what Daniel was preparing, and therefore, she wasn't sure how she should dress for the evening. The indecisiveness was surprising for her, since she was always able to make decisions quickly. Finally, she selected her most comfortable Levi's and a shirt she had just bought at The Gap.

Knowing that she had to deliver her weekly seminar to the American Management Association members at noon, Elaine cut her daydreaming short. This week, she was to lecture about her favorite topic, 'The Customer Lifetime Value,' one of the central themes of Intimate Marketing. She drove to the Marriott Hotel, parked her car in the lot, and strode into the impressive lobby. Taking a few moments to collect herself and regain her serious, authoritative posture, she entered the lecture hall, ready to teach the senior members of the forum a little about Intimate Marketing.

They had scheduled her seminar at one of the most difficult hours, right before lunch, but she knew that she could generate enthusiasm for the subject. She began with her personal story, in which everyone learned that she had been getting her hair styled at the same hairdresser for fifteen years, and the story about the hairdresser segued directly into the seminar topic.

"The customer lifetime value, or CLV," she began, "is the net profit realized from the average new customer over a stated number of years." Then she provided illustrations to prove her point.

"Let's take a hypothetical example. There is a publication called the *Customer Intimacy Journal,* or *CIJ.* Let's say a yearly subscription costs a hundred and fifty dollars. Let's also assume the profit margin from each new subscription is fifty dollars. What is the 'lifetime value' of a *CIJ* subscriber?

"Remember we're talking about a specific time period. The time period must be selected in consideration of your product, the strength of your competition, and several other factors. Concerning the *CIJ,* for example, if it is an accepted fact that the average customer subscribes for four years, then the 'Customer Lifetime Value' in this case is four times fifty dollars, or two hundred dollars. What does all this mean? It means CIJ management will find it worthwhile to invest a hundred dollars today, or even more, for each new customer, because the CLV justifies the investment.

"But, as you can imagine, it's not so simple. If the customer leaves the *Journal* after one year, the paper has lost its initial investment. Here is where experience comes in, on the one hand, and Intimate Marketing, on the other. The greater your knowledge and experience, the more accurately you can gauge the value of investing in new customers. On the other hand, the more effective your Intimate Marketing process, the longer you'll be able to extend the CLV, and subsequently, the customer's value over time. From this, we can conclude that the greater the CLV, the more attractive Intimate Marketing becomes."

Curious thoughts about what the evening might hold threatened to derail her train of thought, but she pushed them aside, regained her composure, and continued.

"In calculating the CLV, it is advisable to consider other influences as well, such as how a customer with 'high lifetime value' impacts the participation of other customers. If, for example, we estimate that for every ten subscriptions we can expect to gain one new subscription through referrals, this additional subscription must be factored into the time equation. In other words, each *Customer Intimacy Journal* subscription contains within itself one tenth of an additional subscription. Since we calculate the 'lifetime value' of a new subscriber as two hundred dollars over four years, there is another tenth worth twenty dollars, and therefore the lifetime value of the customer is actually two hundred and twenty dollars. We can even refine the calculation further.

"With each new subscription, we can raise advertising rates, since advertising rates are a function of total circulation. Data like this can also be quantified and then added into the equation. The example I provided is purely hypothetical, but you can see that, in each organization, the 'customer lifetime value' is the basic premise upon which Intimate Marketing practices are based, and therefore, you must research and consider each customer's real value with as much precision as possible. It is also important to remember that the 'customer lifetime value' is dynamic, and therefore capable of changing from one moment to the next in response to market competition, the company's strength, and the level of its investment. Maybe my hairdresser didn't study marketing, but he succeeded in retaining the same customers for years and years. He understands Intimate Marketing! It is worthwhile for every marketing manager to routinely check the 'lifetime value' of each customer.

"Now, please refer to the handouts, and for the next thirty minutes complete the exercise on 'Customer Lifetime Value.' Afterwards, we will take a short break and then discuss five main strategies to increase CLV."

Elaine felt that she needed this break more than ever. Unlike most days, today she found it difficult to break free from her thoughts, none of which had anything to do with Intimate Marketing. Even while appearing confident in front of an audience of senior managers, she couldn't stop wondering what Daniel was preparing for her this evening. This feeling of losing control and getting carried away was new, frightening, unsettling, and exciting, all at once.

For a few weeks now, Elaine had noticed that one of her students, Art London, a marketing manager who always mentioned his career in four Fortune 500 companies, was sending looks her way, which were hard to misinterpret. Elaine had known him for several years. She also knew he was a forty-two-year-old married man with two children, who was trying, with only partial success, to hide both his baldness and expanding waistline. He was a slick marketing manager in the habit of propositioning his secretaries, a fact that certainly lowered her opinion of him. She thought about his wife, who undoubtedly took primary responsibility for their children and most probably was faithful to him.

As soon as the break began, Art London approached Elaine and demanded, rather aggressively but with a smile, that she tell him how she liked her coffee. "Latte, with one sugar, right?" he asked and didn't even wait for her answer. After a minute, he returned with two cups, one for him and one for her, and gave her his most heart-warming smile. *His secretaries must be sick of him, so he's decided to point his antennae elsewhere,* Elaine thought, with growing revulsion.

But outwardly, she had to be cordial. She politely thanked him, asked him how his wife and children were, and complimented him on his expertise in preparing coffee. The coffee he had prepared really was good. "The company I worked for once has been providing coffee to this hotel for fifteen years now," he bragged.

Not one minute later, he suggested that she would join him for coffee elsewhere—somewhere outside the office *and* the hotel. "I think we'd have many things to talk about," he said. Elaine was forced to tell him that in the coming week she was very busy, but that she would be happy to chat with him online. *Art London is a customer,* she told herself sternly, *and according to Intimate Marketing, I have to please him even above his expectations...but in this case, I must set some limits.*

As the break ended, she handed out a list of the three strategies she would be discussing. "Because the subject is so important," she said to the participants, "I ask that you follow along with me as I discuss each one. Each one of you can select one or more of the three main strategies for increasing every customer's value."

1. Strategy for increasing customer retention

In the past, research has shown that the cost of acquiring a new customer is, on average, five times that of retaining an existing customer. In many industries, today, it costs even more. This strategy aims to help you reduce customer attrition. We will begin with an example:

Let's say that in year one, one hundred of your customers yield a profit of $100 each. So in the first year, you will earn $10,000. If in every succeeding year, you lose half of those customers, you will earn only $5,000 in year two, and $2,500 in year three. Altogether, you will have earned $17,500 from those one hundred customers. Therefore, the 'lifetime value' of your average customer over the three-year period would be $175: $17,500 divided by 100 (assuming for the sake of illustration, we ignore capitalizing on current values).

Further, let's also say that we implement Internet-based e-marketing, to increase customer satisfaction, and to increase the loyalty rate from 50 percent to 60 percent. At this point, the 'customer lifetime value' over the three-year period will be $196 (100 plus 60 plus 36). In other words, your incremental profit over the three years is $21 per customer. If your customer retention activities have cost you, say, $7 per customer, you have earned an additional $14 over the three-year period. By multiplying this increase by your total number of customers, you can calculate the incremental net profit resulting from your Intimate Marketing investment. Perhaps this example is a bit simplistic, but it accurately illustrates how increasing customer loyalty pays off.

2. Strategy for increasing referrals

Word of mouth is considered to be the most effective communication form. Remember—the new generation does not use the Internet…they live there. They eat with Facebook, they sleep with YouTube, they watch TV on their laptop or iPad, and they connect to each other 24-7. They have hundreds of friends online. Some small toddlers say "Google" before they say "Grandma." If you do not play the game with the new rules, you will be out of business soon. It is also worthwhile to remember that the more satisfied the customer, the more effective the word of mouth. But this also applies in reverse: the less satisfied the customer, the more destructive their word of mouth will be to your business. In the age of Internet, the destructive potential is more significant than in the past. Disappointed customers can, and do, spread the word on-line, and within hours, millions of people will know about their experience with your business! Unsatisfied customers can, and they do, build a 'do-not-buy-this-product.com' site, in fifteen minutes, and DESTROY your business with a funny two-minute video they will upload to YouTube, and spread like a virus.

The 'lifetime value' of each existing customer increases, as they bring in new customers. The strategy for increasing referrals employs tactics that lead the customers to believe it is worthwhile to bring in new business. This strategy yields a valuable by-product: a customer who actively markets your business. Such customers become more loyal to your company and, in the process, further compound their own 'lifetime value' as your customer. Before we go to the next strategy we have a unique example to demonstrate the power of referrals and the connected world. I am talking about President Barack Obama.

In 2008, when he ran for president, Obama understood the importance of creating rapport and developing a relationship with potential voters, so he used the Internet to build it. He knew that they would influence the friends of his supporters, so he helped them build their own mini-sites of social networks. Those actions, along with others, helped the Obama team to raise donations of hundreds of millions of dollars, which strengthened the commitment to vote for him in November 2008. You see, Intimate Marketing is the president's choice too… You should remember: today, every customer is your best sales representative. Treat them well, create an intimate relationship with them, and you will be able to stimulate action!

3. Strategy for increasing your share of customers
Because selling more products to existing customers is easier than attracting new ones, the strategy for increasing your share of customers

is based on broadening the range of sales to those already involved in an Intimate Marketing relationship with you.

This strategy relies heavily on broad customer information already collected by the company. You may recall, in Intimate Marketing, we emphasize collecting customer information to help identify and extend the right offer to the right person at the right time. This strategy of increasing the share of customers translates the gathering of customer information into practical reality.

For example, let's assume you manage a baby-products store. You can anticipate customer needs because a) you have records about previous purchases that reveal patterns, and b) you have product information about which items are purchased most frequently, as the babies grow older. This is your opportunity to target your offer to just the right customer with just the right product at just the right time.

One way to apply the strategy of increasing share of customers is to think about products for which there is a universal need. If the customer needs the product, she or he will buy from those who deliver the greatest satisfaction. If, for example, you have a pet, you buy a certain quantity of food on a regular basis. Do you buy it at different stores each time? If so, then apparently, no one supplier has successfully met your specific needs or applied Intimate Marketing principles in a way that attracts you to their store. It might be worthwhile for the store to give you a free dog, if you agree to buy its food from them for the rest of the dog's life.

In many cases, the increase in share of customers is based on repeat sales of a certain product line. Another method is through 'cross-selling,' like selling a shirt to someone who just bought slacks. It is possible, of course, to expand on this idea and sell the same customer matching socks, ties, and jackets. Intimate Marketing makes it easier to increase the range of sales to existing customers, because you have records of their prior *purchases, and therefore you are able to identify which products they are more likely to buy.*

Remember Alfredo, the grocer from Albany, New York? He did not have high-tech. But he had high-touch. The more you add value for your customers, remember them, remember their needs and wants, and create intimate relations based on trust, the more loyal they will be.

When I order a book from websites like Amazon.com, and they send me emails when there is a new book by the same author or on the same topic, I feel they remember me.

Elaine concluded the topic, looked at her participants, stole a quick look at her wristwatch, and closed by saying goodbye to the group until the following week. For homework, she asked them to be prepared to share their own personal experiences to illustrate each point she presented in the list of strategies. Drawing from experience, she knew that next week's session, which would begin with each participant sharing his or her own personal stories, would be both engaging and intriguing. She always enjoyed hearing their stories.

But more than anything, she longed to know what Daniel had in store for her that evening. So she hurried to pack her iPad and belongings into her briefcase,and headed toward the parking lot. In her free hand she carried the printed PowerPoint notes.

Shortly after leaving the building, she sensed that someone was following her. Feeling anxious, she chose not to turn her head and look, but instead kept walking and listening. *Maybe someone else just happens to be leaving now, too,* she reasoned, trying to calm herself. But the farther she walked, the more certain she was that someone really was following her.

Abruptly, she turned her head, and her eyes met the gaze on Art London's smug face. He hurried toward her, taking a long drag on his cigarette and blew smoke rings in her direction. Only inches separated them now. Knowing they were alone, not even the lot attendant was nearby, Art blurted out his personal confession. "I can't take it anymore," he groaned, paying no attention to the look of shock on her face, or her clenched fists.

"Elaine, I'm simply head over heels in love with you. I can't concentrate anymore in your seminar. I just look at you all the time and fantasize that you and I are together in this hotel, but in a different room, say a honeymoon suite with a Jacuzzi and all the available comforts. Elaine, let me take you there. Let me make my love real to you. I'm dying for you; I can't take it anymore."

Elaine was completely blown away. In her short career, this had never happened to her before. From time to time, she'd heard stories and read about situations like this in the paper. It was different when it happened to you personally. Deep down she knew she must pull herself together and run as fast as she could to her car, or maybe toward the lot attendant, to get away from him. She was afraid of this man who was acting like an animal out of control. But her legs felt like stone; they refused to obey her.

In a split second, Elaine chose another strategy. She smiled at Art sweetly and spoke to him soothingly. She patted him on the shoulder in a friendly way, and tried to calm his passion. "Come walk me to my car. I need to get something, and we can talk on the way."

With marked impatience, Art trailed behind her, slightly deflated. As they approached her car, Elaine calculated that she would need about ten seconds to make her escape. As she opened the car door, she felt Art's hand caressing her from behind. Suddenly, she drew on strength she didn't know she possessed. She knocked his hand away, vaulted into her car, stomach churning, and started the engine with a roar, shifting gears and hitting the gas simultaneously. Art London was left standing there, stunned. He obviously hadn't expected his declaration of love to end like this.

It was only when she emerged from the lot and saw the main street awash with sunlight that she allowed herself to take a deep breath. *That was definitely sexual harassment,* she thought. *I've just become one of those sexual harassment victims. Unbelievable! The nerve of the guy!* At the next intersection, Elaine pulled the car to the side to collect herself. She shut her eyes for a few minutes, forced herself to breathe deeply and slowly, straightened her clothes, and knew that, more than anything, she wished that Daniel were there to hug her just now. She not only needed it, she longed for it with all of her heart and soul.

A quick glance at her watch showed that it was a quarter to two. She had five more hours until their date. Elaine decided not to go to the office. She was afraid that, given the incident, she would be too shaken to get anything accomplished there.

* * *

Art London could hardly believe what had happened. Usually, the secretaries at his company stood in line to spend time with him, even though all of them knew he had a family. He had never encountered such an extreme and negative reaction from a woman. True, he had heard that there were women who said No, and meant it. But in his private lexicon, this word did not exist.

Looking down at the ground, he noticed some pages fluttering around the spot where Elaine's car had been parked. He bent down and picked them up. *How to Market Goods and Services Based on the Customer's Lifetime Value,* the heading read. Art London clutched the pages to his chest and inhaled the faint scent of perfume, a maddening reminder of Elaine. With faltering steps, he went back into the hotel, sat down in the lobby, ordered a strong Latte, and tried to understand what had gone wrong with his life.

The words written in Elaine Sherman's own handwriting danced right before his eyes. He didn't know whether or not he would return the notes to her, but in the meantime, he decided that reading them might calm him down. Besides, after what had just happened, he wasn't sure he would be able to show his face in that class again, so at least he could catch up on some of the material.

Your 'customer lifetime value' is, as we've said, a major component of strengthening your Intimate Marketing relationships, Elaine had written.

The customer's lifetime value is directly related to the bottom line of the company, focusing on the marginal profit from each new customer. An advantage of improving Intimate Marketing by focusing on 'lifetime value' stems from the fact that the focus is really on the customer himself. It's nearly impossible to leave the customer out of the equation when working with this system.

It may seem trivial, but honestly, how many times have you implemented an impressive marketing approach that failed because you neglected to consider the most important variable... the customer?

You're probably thinking, "If this is so important, why didn't they teach us this in Marketing 101?" Well, it appears that in many academic institutions, they teach basic marketing concepts. Intimate Marketing, which is based on 'relationship marketing,' belongs to the more modern world. Another explanation as to why so few consider 'customer lifetime value,' is the scarcity of marketing information and data. If you don't capture exact data, using the CLV is almost impossible.

Therefore, before calculating the CLV, you must first draft and implement a plan to gather data on an ongoing basis. Only then will you be able to use the various strategies for increasing customer lifetime value.

You will now be asking yourselves, "So, what is a customer's actual 'lifespan?'" The answer is that in reality, this is unimportant (except in the case where you represent a life insurance company). What is important is the length of time you are willing to invest in using the system as a guide to calculate the cost of investing in new customers.

You should remember that the longer the time period on which you base your 'customer lifetime value,' the greater your risk. For example, if you market health food products and find that your annual profit from an average family is $1,200, simple calculations will tell you that the CLV over five years is $6,000. This is a significant sum, which easily justifies the investment in attracting new families.

Let's look at why it is sometimes risky to calculate 'customer lifetime value' using a longer time frame. What would happen if, after six months, the FDA were to ban some of the products you carry? What would happen if the health-food fad loses momentum? For such situations, it may make sense to consider a shorter time frame when calculating the CLV. How short? That depends on you.

Actually, all life insurance policies marketed by insurance companies are literally based on 'customer lifetime value.' The insurance company 'bets' on you. As strange as it sounds, with an insurance policy, the customers are betting that they will die sooner than when the insurance company thinks they will. In contrast, if you take out an insurance policy at the age of forty and consistently pay the monthly premium for thirty years, the insurance company wins, and in the end, you have paid far more than the amount your survivors would have received had you 'won.'

Let's go back to the health-food example.
If no one had cash flow issues, and if everyone could go to the bank manager and offer future 'customer lifetime value' as collateral, it would be worthwhile to invest as much as $3,000 to attract each new family! Unfortunately, however, the bank will not give you a loan with this type of collateral.

Why is it that 'customer lifetime value' in an insurance company is calculated over many years with almost no risk to the company? Because it is calculated according to 'life expectancy statistics,' which have been collected and analyzed year after year. What every marketer can learn from insurance companies is this: the more trend data you gather over time, the more accurate your estimation will be in calculating 'customer lifetime value.'

If your customers differ substantially from one another in terms of the goods and services they purchase, you will most likely have to calculate 'customer lifetime value' separately for each group. For instance, in a chain store like Wal-Mart, which markets many different products under one roof, there are some customers who primarily buy clothing, and there are other customers who never buy clothing, but occasionally buy electrical *appliances or sports equipment. You would have to calculate customer lifetime value very differently for each of these two groups.*

Art London noticed that his coffee was completely cold. Suddenly, he thought about his own 'customer lifetime value.' What was he worth, really? What value did he have in the eyes of his wife? His children? Elaine? And the question that troubled him most: what value did he have in his own eyes?

He felt great shame about what he had done to Elaine. Sure, in the end, nothing had really happened, no one was hurt physically, and maybe it was possible to insist it had all been a joke. But deep inside he knew there was no humor in it. He had simply lost his head and violated Elaine's dignity, which he really did recognize and appreciate. *What should I do now?* He racked his brain, but no bright ideas sprung forth. He only knew that he needed to apologize, and the sooner the better. He prayed she wouldn't go to the police and lodge a complaint. Business like that was the last thing he needed right now.

Chapter 5

Love in the Mirror

*E*laine Sherman turned the key in her apartment door. A lonely silence awaited her. Suddenly, the thought of Tiger, Daniel's charming, furry friend, came to mind. She had often thought of adopting a cat or dog but had never followed through with it. Now she regretted that she didn't have a cat weaving between her ankles, meowing and purring at her arrival.

She was unable to clear the memory of the day's events from her mind, so Elaine took a long, relaxing shower, letting the hot water and scented soap wash over her shapely body, as her thoughts wandered. Art London's surprise confession about his love for her mixed in her mind with Daniel's silent yearning looks. She thought suddenly about Art's wife—did she love him? Did he love her? What kind of life did they share, and why did he feel the need to flirt with other women? *I wonder how betrayals influence relationships in business*, she thought.

After showering and wrapping herself in a soft, fluffy robe, Elaine made a cup of cinnamon tea and fell into bed. The movie channel featured a romance, which suited her just fine. She drank in the quiet comfort of her home, feeling relaxed and protected. At six o'clock, she decided to get up and start preparing for her date. Although she had no idea what Daniel Marks had in mind for the evening, she wasn't apprehensive. To her surprise, she realized she trusted him completely. Although difficult to admit to herself, she would have been willing to fly to the moon with him.

* * *

At that same hour, Daniel Marks was still at work, busy with his final preparations for the evening he had planned. He reminded himself to buy mineral water for the long trip to Sammy and Lynn's farm in upstate New York.

Sammy, a childhood friend, was waiting impatiently for Elaine and Daniel's arrival. There was already a bowl of fresh fruit placed on a small table next to the gently swaying hammock on the porch of his sprawling farmhouse. Several cats lounged nearby hoping, in vain, to get something to eat.

Daniel returned home just long enough to take a quick shower. He changed from his business attire to jeans and a checkered shirt, quickly brushed his dark hair, and packed some of his favorite CDs in a backpack. He hoped Elaine liked Elton John too. Sharing his favorite music with her was like baring his soul. A moment before leaving, he looked in the mirror. Here and there he noticed a touch of gray hair, but on the whole he was satisfied with his appearance. He wanted very much for Elaine to feel the same.

Just before seven o'clock he stood in front of Elaine's apartment door. It was hard for him to conceal his excitement. This was his first time visiting her apartment—her sanctuary—and he wanted to like it. He wanted it to be homey and warm and was quite sure she had the budget to decorate it tastefully. *I wonder how her bed looks...*but he knew *that* road was far off for now.

Elaine welcomed him dressed in jeans and a soft, colorful blouse. She looked so captivating, so desirable, that he had to actually refrain himself from kissing her. She took his hand, pulled him inside, and seated him on a soft, green easy chair in the living room. There was the scent of fresh flowers in the air, as well as the smell of coffee that Elaine had just prepared.

She gazed at him questioningly. Apparently he was right—she *had* been tormenting herself all day, wondering what their evening together would bring. He decided not to tell her anything just yet. Elaine brought him a cup of coffee (with chocolate chip cookies of course), and placed it in front of Daniel with a smile reserved for someone special. There was no hint of superiority. Daniel was clearly pleased.

"So, how was your day?" he asked, and then inquired about her father. He saw a faint cloud darken her eyes and then disappear. Elaine was thinking about the particularly unpleasant event with Art London and couldn't decide whether or not to share it with Daniel. Her decision was interrupted by an abrupt knock at the door. Elaine tensed; she wasn't expecting any other visitors. Who could it be? With a quick glance through the peephole in the door she saw a FedEx logo. She opened the door, and the messenger handed her a package filled with fancy boxes of coffee. Tucked inside the package was an envelope. *I'm sorry from the bottom of my heart about what happened,* were the words scrawled on the front. Included in the package were the lecture notes she had dropped while escaping from Art. *Excellent material—you are really something,* said the note Art had attached to the pages.

"Do you need some help?" Daniel asked Elaine, who was looking very confused. She closed the door and continued staring at the package of coffee. Daniel understood something was wrong, but chose not to interfere. He waited for Elaine to respond, but she continued to stand there, silent and embarrassed.

Daniel got up from the chair, took her hand, and sat her down next to him. Elaine felt like a small girl holding her father's hand, no longer afraid, because she was with someone strong and capable. "I have to tell you what happened to me today," she began. Daniel raised his eyes to her face, and Elaine began to tell him everything that had taken place that afternoon. Tears streamed down her cheeks as she spoke, and Daniel wiped them away, gently stroking her hair.

He knew that if he had the opportunity, he would deliver a hard and fast punch to Art London's face. But Art London was elsewhere, and Elaine was so close, and so vulnerable and broken. "My coach awaits, princess," he said to her with a big smile, and suggested that perhaps a pleasant ride in the country might help to clear her head. He still didn't mention the destination, revealing only that, in a few hours she would know quite a bit about his childhood. Elaine's tears dried. Daniel could see she was very curious.

Elaine sat in the passenger's seat. Although she was independent and assertive, it was nice to let someone else take charge for a change. They headed north, and eventually, after an hour or so, Elaine began to feel like home was quite far away. She felt somewhat strange, and for the first time since leaving her apartment, she felt a little anxious.

Daniel perceived this and decided to begin his story. "I don't know," he said, "if you've ever felt that you owed someone your life, Elaine. But I owe mine to a guy named Sammy, my best friend since we were both eight years old. We got to know each other when we lived in the same neighborhood in Florida. He went to a different school, but in the afternoons, we would play outside together. We found an abandoned old shack in the woods where we started our secret gang, pretending to be detectives who solved all kinds of mysteries.

"One evening, we were sitting together in the shack. I had brought some candles because there was no electricity. Shortly after I lit one of the candles, it toppled over, hit the floor, and within minutes, the entire shack was consumed in flames. Sammy immediately ran outside, thinking I was right behind him, but I wasn't. I was paralyzed with fear. I couldn't pull my gaze from the flames surrounding me. I felt hypnotized.

"We were both ten years old then. Sammy was in complete control. He yelled to me to run, but I couldn't hear him. So he picked up a large rock and began pounding on the walls of the small shack. When he realized he was getting nowhere, he ran inside and dragged me out after him. Just after making it to safety, the shack collapsed. I never told anyone, not even my parents, about how Sammy saved my life. But Sammy knew exactly how I felt, and from then on, we have been inseparable—true soul mates for life.

"I left to attend University, but Sammy preferred working the land. He's a pioneer at heart, so it was appropriate for him to make that choice. He bought a plot of land in upstate New York and built a beautiful farmhouse on the property. Later, he married Lynn, a girl he met while on a trip to Paris. They have a sweet little daughter named Carrie. I told them about you, and they are anxious to meet you. In fact, that's where we're going. Another—another forty-five minutes, and we'll be there."

Elaine was so riveted by his story that she didn't feel the time passing. Suddenly, it dawned on her that something very intimate had happened between her and Daniel Marks, and she felt great excitement. He had shared with her something he had never told anyone else. He trusted her. Her usual serious expression melted into a sweet smile. *This evening is going to be very special, indeed, maybe even unforgettable,* she thought, and looked forward to their arrival with great anticipation.

The road wound its way through tree-covered hills until they spotted a cluster of lights in the distance. "There's Sammy's farm," Daniel told her, and Elaine saw a new energy light up his eyes. "We take a right here at this dirt road, and we're there," he said more to himself than to Elaine. He felt great joy—knowing this was not just a reunion with two of his best friends, but their first introduction to the woman he liked so much.

Elaine felt a little shy, as the car came to a stop, and Daniel opened the door for her. Lynn was the first to approach, smiling radiantly. She was naturally pretty and extremely warm and friendly looking. Elaine knew at first glance that they would get along well. "Sammy will be here in a second. He's been waiting for you all day," said Lynn.

Little Carrie ran out of the house and tackled Daniel with a hug. It was obvious the two shared a mutual love for one another. She was a sweet, natural-looking child with brown curls and hands that were perpetually full of either mud or chocolate. Daniel could never tell which.

Sammy emerged from the house, and the two gave each other a long, hard hug. They had seen each other just two months ago, but from the way they acted, it might have been much, much longer. Everyone sat beneath a tree, where Sammy and Lynn had refreshments spread out on a picnic table. It was nearly nine o'clock, and the night air was pleasant and quiet, with small, gentle sounds one never hears in the city.

Sammy was updating Daniel on the farm situation, crops and such, and only later did he turn and exchange a few words with Elaine. He looked her up and down and seemed satisfied with what he saw. "I heard that you're a big authority on everything related to marketing and that my good friend Danny has a lot to learn from you," Sammy said to her with a wink. Elaine smiled without answering.

Lynn brought out a light supper: a large green salad; stuffed squash; fresh carrot juice; and brown bread. Dessert was a cheesecake—one of Elaine's favorites. Everything about the evening was very pleasant, and Elaine was beginning to feel attached to these country folk whose lives were so different from her own. *They chose this life,* she thought, *and it looks like they are at peace with their choice.* "Tell me how you met," she asked Lynn and Sammy.

The two looked at each other and laughed. "It all began in Paris, a popular crossroads for young people," Lynn began. "I was working in a youth hostel as a cook and had placed a big pot of cooked vegetables on the kitchen floor. Sammy entered the kitchen, not looking where he was going, and somehow put his foot right into the pot. At first we were both horribly embarrassed, but then we saw the comical side and laughed non-stop for the next half-hour. I even loaned him some clean socks, because all of his were dirty! We had seen each other before, of course, but never had occasion to speak. He always seemed like a nice guy, but it was only because of this crazy accident that I found out just *how* nice."

Sammy smiled and confirmed Lynn's words. He then said to Elaine, "I heard you are an expert in a new marketing methodology. Danny told me about it in great detail." Elaine smiled self-consciously. This evening she had done her utmost *not* to be Elaine, Marketing Expert, but simply Daniel's companion. Sammy persisted, however. "I'd appreciate it if you would just give me a few minutes of professional advice." Elaine had no choice but to agree.

"As Danny probably told you," Sammy said, "we are still trying to make a living from farming and working the land. We've enjoyed reasonable results, although on a limited scale, due to our small size and a shortage of good help. We manage to sell most of what we produce and also supply our own table with food. But in terms of marketing management, I feel like we could be selling more and at more competitive prices."

"Do you have repeat customers?" Elaine asked. Sammy described several small local businesses that routinely bought from them—a school cafeteria and a retirement home among them. "The rest of our produce is sold at the wholesale farmers' market." He mentioned that, in the past, they had tried to make sales agreements with new customers, but they never seemed to last.

"Did you ever ask why these prospective customers preferred to buy elsewhere?" Elaine probed. Sammy admitted that until now he hadn't given it much thought.

"Sammy, I'm inviting you to attend a course I'm giving on Intimate Marketing. I'm sure you would benefit greatly from it. Come to Manhattan next week. I would be honored if you would be my guest," Elaine offered. Sammy promised to do so, starting the following week. In the meantime, she left him with a few points to ponder. "Intimate Marketing is like a romantic attraction. You must continually court your existing customers and work to attract potential customers with all the seriousness of romance. I am sure that if all your crops are as delicious as what we've just enjoyed, you have a lot of untapped potential. I would be happy to give you some advice."

Daniel sat next to her, feeling proud. *She's so smart and quick thinking*, he noted with satisfaction. He looked at his watch; it was already midnight. He knew that Sammy and Lynn had to get up early the next day and he, too, didn't want to arrive at International Airlines bleary-eyed in the morning. He gently grasped Elaine's hand and gestured that they needed to head back. Elaine got up, expressing a heartfelt goodbye to Sammy and Lynn, and asked them to kiss Carrie for her, since she was already in bed.

The return trip was tranquil. The city freeway was so much faster in the evening without traffic jams, she noted. She couldn't remember what they talked about on the long way home. She only remembered Daniel's pleasant voice sharing all kinds of stories about his life. She snuggled down in the soft seat and even fell asleep momentarily. Tomorrow would be a full day...

* * *

Daniel's car coasted to a stop across from Elaine's building. He walked her to the door of her apartment, but he didn't dare go inside. He and Elaine looked at each other in silence. Suddenly, Daniel remembered that he had something for her. He handed her an envelope, saying, "This is for your dad." In it were the details he had collected on IA's best deals for upcoming trips, including vacation packages to the French Riviera, Shanghai, and an interesting package to Jerusalem, the holy city for Christians, Muslims, and Jews. He dared to dream that, someday, he would take the Frequent Flyer member standing next to him to one of those places. *Maybe for a honeymoon…*

Elaine took the envelope from him and promised to deliver it at the first opportunity. She didn't quite know how to say goodbye, but she didn't object as Daniel's handsome face slowly moved closer to hers. He kissed her on her cheek and on her closed eyes, and then he found her lips. Elaine yielded to his warm kiss. Daniel felt Elaine's body move and his excitement was hard to contain. *Where will we end up?* he wondered.

Elaine was the first to disengage from the kiss, after what seemed like several long, sweet minutes to both of them. She opened her door and then looked at him.

"You know, Elaine, I wanted to play my favorite music for you. I even brought some CDs, but I didn't have a chance..." he faltered. Elaine put a finger on his mouth to silence him, took him by the hand, and led him straight to her bedroom.

Daniel tried to say something, but Elaine took control of the situation. Again, she brought her finger up to his mouth and whispered, "Shhh." She pressed her body against his, brought her eager lips to his mouth, and flicked her tongue in an intimate movement that left no room for debate. Daniel drew back, only to bury his face in the warmth of her neck, planting soft kisses from her shoulder to her ear, sending shivers through Elaine's body. Slowly and smoothly Daniel lifted her shirt, pressing his hands against her warm flesh. As he reached around her to open the clasp of her bra, Elaine began unbuttoning his shirt and unfastening his belt. In what seemed like an instant, their bodies, free of barriers, converged into one beneath the warmth of Elaine's goose down comforter.

As Daniel explored Elaine's body with his own, she dissolved in his arms, closed her eyes, and bathed in the ecstasy of their union. Every fiber of her body and soul was alive with Daniel. She couldn't recall the last time she had given herself so readily—and so completely. As they joined together, she wrapped her legs around him and held him tight wishing the moment would last forever. Daniel was lost in his own thoughts. He couldn't help but think how soft and yielding she was—so different from the assertive, capable woman he had first met at the marketing seminar. At last, he had reached into her depths and found the gentle, vulnerable woman he had known was there. He felt her give in to him—felt her body melt into his own, until he could no longer tell where one ended and the other began. Moving together to the crest of the wave that carries lovers to another place and time, they released, shuddered slightly, and limp with spent passion, sweat and contentment, loosened their grip on one another, smiling.

At 6:20 the next morning, the sun's rays woke Daniel. He jumped out of bed. He had to be in a meeting at eight. Elaine was still sleeping. He found some red lipstick on the night table, and used it to draw a big red heart on the mirror. He bent over her, hoping she was awake after all, then kissed her on the forehead and quietly left the apartment.

Daniel lingered a few moments outside Elaine's closed door and then went quickly down the stairs. The trip home to 58th street seemed stranger than ever. The night replayed in his memory. *Sammy brings me luck,* he thought. He went hurriedly into his apartment, showered, and dressed in record time, and went out to join the rat race of commuters heading to work.

Chapter 6

Intimacy in Marketing

Elaine was awakened by the telephone at nine o'clock in the morning. It took her a few seconds to adjust to the surroundings after opening her eyes. Her clothes were thrown in a heap on the floor next to her bed. She didn't even bother to hunt for the cordless phone, which by now had stopped ringing. She smiled, remembering the previous night. Then she noticed the red heart on the mirror. The phone began ringing once again, interrupting her thoughts. Maybe it was Daniel. She pounced on the black cordless phone and pushed the button. It was her father on the line.

"I passed by your place last evening dear, and didn't see any lights. I hope you had a good time," he said, and Elaine could almost hear the wink in his voice. "I took a ride with Daniel to visit some of his friends," she explained. Although she really didn't appreciate her parents getting involved in her life, she had learned not to let it upset her. They meant well. She told her father that Daniel had prepared a list of destinations recommended for Frequent Flyer and proposed that he stop by her office later that afternoon to pick it up.

Elaine, knowing she had an important consulting session coming up in about two hours, gathered her presentation material and took her iPad to bed, along with a cup of mint tea. She enjoyed working in bed like that. It made her feel pampered while still making efficient use of the time.

Elaine mentally reconstructed the night's events and decided to let Daniel make the next move. *Now that he's acquired a 'customer,' let's see how he continues to attract her,* she thought. But since she had to be in top form for this upcoming meeting, she put fantasies about Daniel aside.

The material about which she was to speak that day was fairly complex: *The Most Effective Ways to Use a Customer Database.* For the most part, the information was focused on several basic principles for maximizing the ability to predict customer behavior. In short, the model was called *"RFM" for Customer Activation.*

> *The "R" stands for recently, based on the likelihood that a customer who has purchased from you once will buy from you again. The conclusion: try to sell to 'hot' customers again. They make good prospects.*

Elaine liked her examples and kept reading her document:

> *Assume that a customer recently purchased a baby crib. The chance that he or she will buy other baby products is greater than someone who hasn't made a recent purchase.*

> *Another example: a customer who is remodeling his bathroom and purchases bathroom fixtures from you is more likely to buy other bathroom accessories than someone who hasn't yet visited your store.*

Of course, the 'recently' factor isn't the only determinant of future sales. But if it helps, why not learn to profit from it? First, you must consider each sale as a segue to the next sale. Extend a special offer to purchasers of specific products, or give them information on other related products. The expense of doing so is minimal, compared to the potential increase in sales. The more experience you have and the more sophisticated your methods, the greater your accuracy in targeting the right 'repeat purchase product.' If, for example, you own an Internet-based music store, you can ask customers purchasing music to tell you what kind of music they like. Then you can offer them the opportunity to buy and download more of what your customers are looking for. Let's say you buy a Boston Symphony Orchestra piano concert album through a company such as Amazon. After you click on the music that you want, the site could then take you to more classical music that you might be interested in purchasing.

Elaine liked the next two ideas and kept reading her own notes:

After Sales Service and Before Next Sales Service.
Instead of providing after sales service to your customers (whose acronym is ASS), you should provide service before the next sale (whose acronym is BNS, or bonus). In this way, it would be easy to remember how to treat clients.

The 'F in the RFM model stands for frequency, based on the assumption that the more frequently a customer does business with you, the greater the chance she will return again. The consistency creates a habit and strengthens the commitment. The conclusion: each time your customers make a purchase, you should view it as another opportunity to sell to them.

If you collect data on your customers and document the details of their purchases, you'll be able to categorize them on the basis of buying frequency. The assumption is that those in the habit of doing business with you will probably continue. Therefore, it is worthwhile to focus on customer retention. Direct-marketers and Internet-based companies have found it worthwhile to target direct marketing offers to their best customers.

The rule is that if you sort your customer files into five groups, based on purchasing frequency, and send a marketing offer to every customer, on average, the response will double from group to group. That is, the response rate from the highest frequency group will be double that of the second highest, and so on. Continuing the calculation, you will find that the most frequent buyers will net an average response rate sixteen times greater than that of the lowest group. You should read it again: the most frequent buyers will net an average response rate sixteen times greater than that of the lowest group.

You can also apply this rule for the first letter of RFM—recently. With recent buyers, too, the proportion doubles on average, from one group to the next.

When you begin developing selling strategies based on RFM, follow these rules with caution, at least in the beginning. Listen to your common sense based on your personal experience and your gut feelings. The most critical step is tracking all results. Doing so will help you to understand why some methods work better than others do.

Clearly, there is a connection between recency and frequency. Remember that it is always preferable to sell to a customer who has made a recent purchase or who does business with you often. If you sold to a new customer yesterday, he becomes a 'fresh, hot' prospect for future purchases. So, you may ask, "Which customers have more potential: the thousand customers who made purchases last month or the top one thousand of your most frequent customers?" There is no definitive answer, except the one that your own experience provides. One thing remains constant: the customer who buys often and who has made a recent purchase presents the best opportunity for future sales.

The telephone rang, breaking Elaine's deep concentration. It was Daniel, sounding very happy she had answered the phone. Daniel had already been in his office working for quite a while but told her, that he felt like he was walking on air.

"Me too," replied Elaine. "I really enjoyed last night."

"I'm in my office and I'm not alone, so I'll be quick and non-romantic. Is eight o'clock okay for tonight?" he asked. Elaine remained indecisive for a moment, thinking that maybe their meetings were getting too intense too quickly, but she couldn't resist. There was no doubt that she wanted to see, touch, and smell Daniel tonight as much as he wanted to see her. "Okay, tonight at eight, I'll come to *your* place, with three of my favorite old CDs, which I also have in MP3 and their vinyl records," she said.

"And I'll make some Italian food." Daniel surprised her. She had no idea he was able to cook. "Cooking Italian is relatively simple," he said, rather modestly. "Do you care for lasagna or fettuccine?"

When Elaine said she'd have whichever was safer, Daniel laughed. "I'm already counting the minutes until I see you," he said.

Elaine was quiet for a moment. "Me too... and by the way, I loved the heart you drew, but it won't wash off my mirror!" Daniel blew her a kiss over the phone and hung up.

Elaine shut her eyes for a minute, trying to prolong her enjoyment of the romantic conversation. Then she collected herself and returned to her notes and started to read the third point in the RFM model: 'M' for money.

The assumption is that the more money a customer spends, the greater the likelihood of repeat purchase. The conclusion: the higher the total value of a customer's purchase, the more worthwhile it is to target that customer again.

In most cases, we can say that the more expensive the item, the greater the customer's risk. People tend not to buy expensive items from a company they don't trust for service. In contrast, one could be tempted to buy an expensive item on sale, because the price (and therefore the risk) is lower. When risk is low, buying is more impulsive and spontaneous. This is where the third factor comes into play: the monetary factor.

The more a customer spends with you, the more he trusts you. Remember that a main component of Intimate Marketing is reliability. A customer who has expressed trust by buying from you presents a greater opportunity for future purchases. Here again, you can divide your database into several groups, according to monetary purchase value, to decide which customers make the best prospects.

A few notes worth remembering:

- There is a connection between the monetary factor and the other two factors. Those who bought recently and buy from you frequently will, in all probability, spend significantly more money.
- There is a significant difference between the purchase price and gross profit from each sale. It may be that you actually profit more from less expensive items with a higher profit margin. You can use your own calculations to determine whether it is better to target customers who trust you enough to buy expensive products (perhaps at a lower margin) or to target those who spend less, and maybe shop less often, but tend to purchase products with a higher markup. You may also combine both strategies by 'pushing' those products with a higher margin to customers who have expressed trust in you, and who will do business with you more frequently.

The RFM model can be applied in several ways. With more experience, you can modify these concepts to most appropriately meet your needs. For example, there are two ways to apply the monetary factor. You can analyze the data, either by the most recent purchase totals, or by cumulative totals over a definitive time period (which provides an interesting relationship between purchase totals relative to frequency data).

A supermarket is a good example of how this analysis can be useful. By performing this analysis, the store can determine whether all customers who spent $400 over the last month spent it in one, two, or ten trips, and whether the total amount spent in each trip differed significantly. Should you appeal to all customers in the same way? Ultimately, that depends upon the store's strategy. If only monthly purchases are of interest, all customers in that group would be viewed as one. But if management wants to develop 'customer lifetime value' with more specific marketing tactics, they will need to differentiate between the groups by customizing the offers. For example, for customers who stock up early in the month, supplementing in between with perishables (like milk), your goal may be to increase their purchase of non-perishable items during their primary shopping trip.

In contrast, the shopper who spends $100 a week may be encouraged to increase the range of purchases each week, focusing more on buying in greater quantities at the beginning of the month. The goal for them is to reduce the likelihood that they will need to replenish items in between from competitive stores.

For yet another type of customer who buys produce and other perishables elsewhere, you can offer free door-to-door delivery every few days. Some more advanced grocers are even promoting Internet shopping with home delivery.

Why is RFM analysis so effective? Because it is based on applying knowledge about customer behavior—specifically, predicting future actions by analyzing past behavior. Clearly there is no guarantee of success, but it is important to note that Intimate Marketing, which is based, in *part, on data gleaned from RFM, is a much more effective approach than segmenting market data by other demographic or psychographic data.*

Elaine left her notes and decided to prepare for her appointment. She filed away her thoughts about last night and her upcoming date with Daniel somewhere in the 'sweet thoughts file,' in order to focus more clearly on her goal. She knew that if she succeeded in convincing the managers with whom she was meeting today to apply Intimate Marketing principles, it would not only earn her respect and professional recognition, but also ensure her more of the type of engagements she was seeking to attract. Since she too applied Intimate Marketing practices with her own customers, she felt certain that she would soon build her clientele with the right type of clients.

After dressing and applying light makeup, she got into a yellow cab and asked the young driver to take her directly to Fifth Avenue at Central Park South, The Plaza Hotel, where the meeting was to take place. A serious traffic jam took her by surprise since it was unusual for this hour of the day. So while waiting, Elaine sank deep into thought about an article she had read: *Turning Lost Customers into Gold.*

In the article, the marketing expert said:

While investigating customer attrition, I discovered some surprising facts. Most of my customers were surprised and happy that the supplier was trying to understand their needs and problems in an effort to increase their satisfaction. I also learned that many customers have great ideas about service and products. Actually, more than 80 percent of successful new products comes from customers' ideas and suggestions. I also noticed that my clients were oblivious even to the most serious problems with their own customers. In some cases, the customers they planned to survey were, in fact, "ex-customers!" Management from the company requesting the research didn't even know it.

Survey results indicated that loyal customers spend more, make more recommendations to new customers more often, and move to the competition less often than new customers do. Most importantly, I discovered that with every successive year that a customer remains loyal, their contribution to overall profit increases. This profit translates into exponential income growth.

It is important to note that companies earn higher profits from a customer with whom it does business for ten years, than from ten customers who do business elsewhere after just one year. When a customer leaves, he takes the income potential with him. Moreover, customers generally leave because they are dissatisfied, and dissatisfied customers personally tell an average of ten others about the problems they experienced with your company, and they share it online with more than 100 Facebook and other social network friends. You can't always calculate the damage, but every company must strive to eliminate customer attrition by keeping each profitable customer happy and satisfied. One research project found a 25-, 50-, and even 100-percent increase in profits from various companies, after reducing customer attrition rate to a mere five percent.

Elaine liked the approach described at a CRM conference she had recently attended about striving to reduce customer attrition to zero. The speaker described a revolutionary strategy. Instead of focusing on attracting new customers, the organization should focus on its most important asset: loyal and committed customers. *The value of these assets should be quantified and included in the yearly balance statement along with expenses, stock, income, etc. Tracking the customer attrition rate confirms that even the smallest decrease in attrition can double and triple profits,* said the speaker.

"One hundred percent customer commitment is your goal," Elaine recited to herself. "Before a company announces that it is really satisfying its customers, it must ask those customers what, if anything, the company can do to improve the relationship. Collecting this information, and acting upon it, will create a win-win situation for everyone—the customers, the employees, the stockholders and the organization."

Chapter 7

Kama Sutra

*E*laine was glad when she finally arrived at the Plaza after the traffic eased up. She was thankful she had allowed enough time to arrive at the meeting early, despite the traffic jams.

She saw that she still had thirty-five minutes before the meeting was to begin, so she decided to sit at the newly restored Oak Bar at The Plaza. She pulled her booklet out of her briefcase and began reading another section in her notes: *Regaining Lost Customers*. She knew she could use some examples in her upcoming seminar.

The typical company loses an average of 30 percent of its customers each year. The cost of each lost customer depends on the business. But if we multiply that 30 percent by the cost of acquiring a customer, or by the income generated by just one customer, we can estimate how much the loss of customers costs us each year.

Here's an example: A local supermarket estimated that the average value of a certain type of customer was $2,000 in annual gross sales. This store had one thousand such customers. If the supermarket loses 20 percent, or two hundred of these customers, their yearly income drops by $400,000! If these are the numbers for a local supermarket, you can imagine the impact on a large manufacturer!

A few years ago, a survey was conducted with two hundred well known companies, focusing on information they collected on both customer attrition and attraction costs. Results showed that only 11 percent of the companies actually knew the 'lifetime value' of a customer. Most did not know their customer attrition rate, and 90 percent of them did not have the tools to detect which customers they were likely to lose.

There are several legitimate reasons that veteran customers generate such high profits. First, the cost of acquiring new customers is very high, particularly when compared with the lower cost of retaining customers. Second, the better your customers know you, the more they buy. Likewise, the better you know your customers, the easier it is to satisfy them. In a consulting firm, for example, it is common knowledge that the cost of maintaining customers drops during the second year of the relationship. Most expenses in the first-year stem from learning what your customer wants and which approach they prefer.

Moreover, you can demand a higher price from a loyal customer. Many prefer to pay more to someone they know than to save a little by doing business with someone they don't know. One survey found that 75 percent of customers queried were buying from businesses that gave them excellent service, even though some of those providers charged higher prices. When you encourage your clients to invest time and emotion in your service and with your company, the chance that they will leave you for a small sale is slight.

In order to prevent customer attrition, you need to establish an information system. Obviously, not all attrition can be eliminated, and in fact, trying to keep every customer is unrealistic, since not every customer is profitable. In order to know which customers are profitable, companies need an effective information system to track and analyze customer activity, and then make adjustments based on their findings.

An information system requires the following components:

- **A method for listening to customers**—their opinions regarding your company, problems they may be experiencing, or reasons for taking their business elsewhere. It can also be a way to gather feedback from those who have taken their business elsewhere.

- **Hotlines** through which managers can listen to customers' complaints and responses.

- **Benchmarking** to find out what other companies do to retain (or lose) their customers.

- **A method for collecting employee data**—formally and informally—using tools such as customer surveys and focus groups designed to find out how customers view their relationship and service with the company.

A company's information system should be accessible to all employees. Results should be shared company-wide through intranet, reports, meetings, etc. The medium is unimportant. The goal is to distribute information and integrate it into strategic planning and daily operations.

You can institutionalize procedures for collecting customer feedback in many ways. Hold regular conversations with at least three customers a week. Speak with one satisfied customer, one dissatisfied customer, and one who's indifferent. Hold scheduled conversations with customers just after they have made a major purchase. Conduct weekly meetings with at least three managers who have direct customer contact, and solicit second-hand feedback through sales people, marketers, and service representatives. Give each employee an opportunity to gain experience in customer contact by inviting customers to visit your facility and express their views.

If your organization is losing customers, it is worthwhile to identify the causes and work quickly to resolve them. You may be surprised to learn that customers often report the main reason for leaving is not high prices or poor-quality products, but inferior service. Therefore, customer service is the first place to investigate when trying to identify failures in meeting customer satisfaction.

Elaine glanced at her watch and saw that she had a few more minutes remaining before her meeting. She decided to continue reading. The heading on the next page was: *The customer is not always right...but he is the customer.*

One of the most important elements of superior service is courteous and timely attention to customer complaints. If you are a senior manager in a large company, you should realize that only a small percentage of all customer complaints ever reach your desk. If, for example, a customer complains about an unfamiliar deduction on his bank statement, he will ask the bank clerk with which he is most familiar. Few will address their complaint to the branch manager. If the clerk resolves it, the issue will likely be put to rest.

Research has shown that only one out of hundreds of customer complaints in a large company ever reaches senior management. This is termed the 'iceberg phenomenon' concerning customer complaints, since senior management is only aware of the tip of the iceberg. All others are generally resolved at lower levels, and managers rarely hear of them. Unfortunately, as a result, senior management often overestimates the level of customer satisfaction.

What can you do? First of all, make sure each complaint or appeal, as well as the outcome, is documented. In addition, make sure that this documentation is made available to senior management.

If you investigate lost customers, you will discover that most never complained, but rather voted with their feet. When discussing customer loyalty with the company, you will learn that those who complain are actually your most loyal customers. They exhibit trust and desire to continue doing business with the company by making known the company's shortfalls, because they believe you will try to address them.

Let's say, for example, that a customer reserved a certain car from your rental agency, but when he came in to pick it up, the only car left was much smaller than what he had requested; the car he had reserved simply wasn't there. To keep him as your client, an agent could take him home, deliver a car even larger than what he requested to his house within two hours, and provide all of these services free of charge. This shows that you care, and this is how you keep customers.

So, who are your most loyal customers? Those who complain and see their problems quickly resolved. The longer a company delays resolution, the more dissatisfied customers become. Among those who complain and feel that resolution was slow, the level of satisfaction is an average of 25 percent lower than those whose complaints were resolved quickly.

Sometimes a company feels the problem was resolved quickly, but the customer believes otherwise. You think that resolving the problem in one day is more than reasonable, but the customer thinks it should have been addressed within an hour. As a result, she loses trust in the company. The conclusion: it is worthwhile to find out what customer expectations are concerning problem resolution. All it takes is a simple question posed by the service representative: "Will it be sufficient if we resolve the problem by this time tomorrow (or whenever) or is this urgent?" Remember that customers who file complaints and receive immediate attention will be most loyal. Therefore, it is worthwhile in the framework of Intimate Marketing to create an atmosphere that encourages customer feedback. Each complaint you receive and resolve satisfactorily represents profit for the company.

In terms of 'customer lifetime value,' remember that a disappointed customer has a negative influence, because dissatisfied customers share their disappointment with far more people than satisfied customers share their satisfaction.

Elaine finished reading and went straight to the meeting room where the executives of Dor Business Intelligence were waiting for her. The general manager introduced her to those present, and she smiled somewhat shyly in response. Most of them were old enough to be her father. The courteous CEO requested that everyone give her their undivided attention, since from now on, she was a participant in the company's 'guerrilla marketing' forum.

Naturally, the meeting was successful. The next session with that forum was scheduled for the following month. Elaine went to catch a cab, glancing back periodically to be sure no one was following her. The memory of the traumatic attack by Art London still made her quite uneasy.

"Hi, honey, when we can meet?" asked her father when he called her iPhone.

"I'll be at my office in another hour, if you can see me then. I'll have some hot chocolate waiting for you," Elaine answered her father fondly. In the last few years, she had been trying to be more sensitive with him, even when he tried occasionally to interfere in her private life. Right now, she was happy to see him and just hoped he wouldn't be too inquisitive about her affairs.

David Sherman was glad to get the list of vacation deals that International Airlines was offering in the coming months. He asked Elaine where she thought he ought to take her mother, for whom his illness had been difficult. Elaine didn't know what to say, since all the destinations looked equally wonderful. To tell the truth, she wouldn't mind flying off somewhere for a few days herself. She didn't want to go alone, of course.

"I understand the young man from IA is still in the picture," said her father in a half-question. Elaine admitted that they were going out and that she was enjoying his company. "He seems like a really nice guy," her father continued, "but don't ever fully trust people you hardly know. External appearance and gentlemanly manners can be misleading."

Elaine was surprised by his reservations, even though she knew he said it mostly out of concern for his oldest daughter. "I know," she said, and they parted with a smile and a warm hug.

Elaine began reviewing the material piled on her desk from the last three days—three days that had held some of the most intimate experiences of her life, figuratively and literally. Her assistant, Allen, was as dependable as a rock, and knew how to keep things running smoothly during her periodic absences. He now handed her a pink envelope with a rose attached to it, saying, "This just came by messenger."

Elaine closed the door behind her. *To the best lecturer I know, from a student who wants to learn more and more,* was written on the attached note. Daniel just signed it with a big *D*. Elaine smiled. She loved these little gestures and tried to think how she could reply in kind.

Contrary to her typical behavior, Elaine did not make it through the entire pile, because she had a sudden yearning to go home and to rest for a while before her date with Mr. D. She didn't eat anything so that she would have more room for his lasagna, or fettuccine as the case might be. She closed her eyes and tried to imagine the smell of Daniel's body.

The telephone rang, putting an end to her train of thought. "This is your new farmer-friend," said the voice on the line, and Elaine recognized Sammy. "When can I start that course you invited me to?" he asked.

Elaine consulted her iPad for a minute and saw that there was a relevant lecture the following day. "Tomorrow I'm speaking about an exciting subject. I call it, the '*Kama Sutra* of Marketing!'" she said.

"*Kama Sutra*? Isn't that the ancient Hindu book widely considered to be the standard work on human sexual behavior with all the impossible positions in it?" asked Sammy playfully.

"Very unoriginal, Sammy. Everyone who has heard me speaking on the subject has made the same joke. Are you coming tomorrow at three, or not?"

"Of course, I'm Kama, I mean coming!"

Elaine was happy to hear from Sammy. She still needed encouragement and approval once in a while, and if Sammy was willing to leave his farm to come and listen to her lecture, he must think she was really worth his time.

All the way home, Elaine thought about how she could surprise Daniel. Suddenly, she spotted a small, but attractive pet store. She stopped the car and went in. If she found something for Tiger, Daniel's beloved cat, he and Tiger would both be pleased. She selected a soft woolly toy from the items the salesman showed her—a favorite among pampered kittens, according to the manufacturer. *I'll add a cute note,* she thought, *and that will be my little gift.*

At seven-fifteen that evening, when she was getting dressed to meet Daniel, her iPhone rang. "Elaine, I'm really sorry. Something came up and I won't be able to make it tonight. We'll talk tomorrow, okay? I'm really very sorry," Daniel said in a rush.

Elaine was alarmed. "What happened?" She tried to ask him.

"I can't talk now. Don't worry. I must go now. I'll call you." He hung up. Elaine tried calling his cell phone, only to get the recorded voice on Daniel's answering service, annoying and mechanical.

Elaine felt uneasy. She was sincerely worried about him, but she was also surprised and a little hurt that he didn't feel the need to let her in on what was happening. *Maybe something happened at work that needs his immediate attention…or…maybe there is something to what my dad told me? Maybe I have to slow down a bit, try to get to know Daniel better, before I get so emotionally involved. Maybe he was scared about what happened between us last night and is afraid of commitment. But, on the other hand, he sent me the note with the rose.* She argued internally with herself, getting nowhere.

She wanted to talk with Norma, but as always, her call was routed to the electronic voice mail. She became aware of a growing hunger, so she opened the refrigerator and peered in. The choices were limited, but she had no desire to go out alone to a restaurant, and ordering pizza didn't seem very appealing either. Hungry and confused, she stretched out on her bed and fell asleep.

Chapter 8

Contact

*W*hen Elaine awoke the next morning, her first thoughts were about Daniel's behavior the previous night. *If he didn't think it appropriate to confide in me, then he can't really expect me to spend time thinking about him,* she thought. Pushing her thoughts aside, she got dressed for a series of morning meetings and her afternoon seminar.

At two forty five that afternoon, while organizing her notes in her lecture room at the hotel, she felt a light tap on her shoulder. Sammy stood there, smiling and holding a big sack of his farm's best produce.

"Thank you very much," said Elaine, with obvious pleasure. "You just saved me a trip to the grocery store, since I just finished the last of my veggies." She debated whether or not to ask Sammy if he knew anything about what was going on with Daniel, or if he knew what had happened yesterday. Then she thought better of it. Daniel needed to tell her directly, so there was no point in bringing Sammy into the picture.

Approaching the platform, Elaine began her lecture. "Today, we have a subject you will all love: 'the law of contact' from the '*Kama Sutra* of Marketing.'" Sammy was glad he had come. *Contact? Who doesn't like that?* he thought.

"Those of you who are thinking we are going to engage in erotica are sorely mistaken," Elaine continued. "Instead, we will discuss seven rules that will help you keep your customers forever. If you apply these seven rules, your chances will be much greater of keeping your customers faithful, encouraging them to buy more products, to tell their friends about you, and in short, to contribute to increased profits. So let's review them one at a time."

Elaine started with some drama: she put on some tango music from Argentina, asked the audience to listen closely, let the music fade out, and then she began:

1. Each contact must satisfy both parties.

As in love, both partners must enjoy the relationship. In our case, if you want your customer to complete a questionnaire designed to evaluate how well you deliver a service, you must 'reward' him or her for taking the time to do it. You will profit from the information, right? Your customer should also profit from being your 'consultant!'

You can either tell your customers up front what's in it for them, or you can surprise them. I'll give you an example. An Italian food products company created a website and applied the principle that every contact must satisfy both parties. When customers log onto their site and provide their names and addresses, they receive discount coupons for various products. In addition, there are a number of activities in which customers may participate, as well as receive recipes for fancy Italian dishes.

I'll give you another example. A contact can also mean sending a greeting card every holiday season. Up to this point, you have only invested money. But you could also attach a self-addressed, stamped postcard on which you ask customers to write their 'wish list' from you for the coming year.

Even if you receive only a few responses, the information will be useful. With each customer contact, try to learn one new thing about them. If a customer calls you to complain, take advantage of the opportunity to treat her with superb care. Chances are you will be rewarded for your efforts—for example, a referral to a potential new customer.

Remember: if either partner feels uncomfortable, there may be no justification for the relationship to continue, just as in life!

Let's go to the second rule:

2. Be diligent about maintaining maximum discretion.
How many times have you gotten angry at a friend who spread a secret you had shared in confidence with him or her? You lost your trust in that friend, right? Well, remember the second rule of 'the law of contact': **All customer information must be kept confidential.** *Guarantee the customers that whatever they tell you will be used only for your purposes, in order to serve them. Never turn the information into sellable merchandise.*

For example, many companies promise customers who supply their email address that the information will not be passed on to any other party. Remember that your "word" is an asset. Don't betray your customers.

And she continued:

3. Be diligent about maintaining frequent contact.
They say there was this sex therapist who, at the end of each lecture, did a survey of his participants regarding their frequency of sexual intercourse. After seeing a few raised hands from those who indicated they engaged in sex at least three times a week, he asked, "Who has sex only once a year?" In the back row, someone raised his hand with excitement. In answer to the lecturer's question as to why he was so happy about it, he answered, "Today's the day!"

Well, your customers ab-so-lute-ly hate to hear from you only when you need them. They detest getting an email or a phone call only when you want to sell them something or renew their subscriptions or policies.

Sammy liked the way Elaine emphasized this point. She continued:

Your customers are wild about contact. They want lots of attention. They want lots of feeling! They don't care how much you know; they want to know how much you care!

Therefore, one of the central principles of Intimate Marketing is planned contact. Divide your customers into groups, according to their importance to your business, and then plan the time and nature of contact you will initiate with each one in advance. The more important a customer is to you, that is, the higher the customer lifetime value, actual or potential, the more worthwhile it is to invest time and money to satisfy her or him on an ongoing and consistent basis.

But today's customers live in a world full of stimuli and temptations. They will not be satisfied with lots of contact and attention; they also want and expect variety.

"This is the fourth rule."

4. Be diligent about varying the contacts.
Customers want to be 'wowed' each and every time.

She switched a PowerPoint slide, and everybody could see the new acronym for 'wow.'

W = What are your dreams/needs/wants/desires?
O = Over-deliver!
W = What else do you need/want/desire?

Do not let the customer think your contact is an automated response. Do not create a response system that relies on routine and predictability! Vary the manner and timing of your contact. 'Wow' them! Remember: if you don't wow, it's ciao!

The more you nurture the customer with a variety of contact, the more she or he will think you are making a serious investment in the relationship. By the way, the more you consider the customer when planning how to make contact, the greater the chance they will want to maintain that contact with you.

If customers learn that each time they hear from you, they will profit in some way (financially or otherwise), they will be happy when you make contact and may even open your email first before the rest of their inbox emails. If customers know that you phone, not only to sell them something, but also to assist them in some way, they will be happy to take the call.

Remember that while an annual customer event is great, it will never make up for lack of attention the other three hundred, sixty-four days of the year. In many ways, it is similar to a husband who pampers his wife only on her birthday and cheats on her the rest of the year. If you succeed in remembering the 'rule of variety,' you can take advantage of every customer contact by learning more about her or his needs, ambitions, and problems that will help you to identify more opportunities to meet customer requests.

"Who would like to play with me?" Elaine paused in her lecture to ask. Nearly all the participants raised their hands. Elaine asked four attendees, one in each corner of the room, to stand and repeat one rule each, and then describe how they could apply them in their own business. Afterwards, she called each of them to the podium and gave them a gift—a wooden tool for a scalp massage. "Each time you use it, or ask your partner to use it on you, remember the 'law of contact,'" she said with a smile. Sammy loved how she broke her routine. *I wonder how she makes contact,* he thought. *Does she know about variety? Does she know how to adapt her marketing ideas at home?*

"Since you all remembered so well," Elaine cut through his thoughts, "we'll move on to the fifth point which, incidentally, is related to memory:"

5. Remember the history of each customer contact.
How would you feel if your good friends didn't remember important details about you and your family like birthdays, your children's names, or your hobbies? Your customers provide a great deal of information and expect you to remember. See how customer information flows in your organization. Does it originate with the sales staff? If so, what happens when a sales representative leaves the company? Is the information passed along to someone else? Create a system within your organization for gathering and documenting important customer information on a regular basis.

I'll let you in on a secret: If you can convince your customers to take the time and effort to teach you what they want, how they want it, and why, they will be more likely to remain loyal to you. Sometimes, customers share personal information with you either through an informal conversation or a comment card. In many cases, you know these customers better than they know themselves. Let's look at an example.

Let's say you are a travel agent and you have a customer named Joseph. You know from experience (and even from his complaints), that Joseph prefers to fly business class, that he hates long flights, and that he expects a hotel room with a spacious bed. You even know that Joseph refuses to stay on the sixth floor! He expects to receive his flight schedule printed out in detail, with four copies. You know how to serve him, because he's been teaching you for a long time. By now, he takes these little things for granted. If he were to take his business to another travel agent, Joseph would have to re-teach the new agent everything. Why would he leave you, if you already attend to his unique needs? Living in an Internet world means he can book his next vacation on many online travel sites, but in many cases, saving a few dollars won't be enough of an incentive to justify the convenience and peace of mind your service provides.

Be diligent about remembering your customers' quirks, and your competition will have a hard time luring them away from you.

Elaine then asked, "Who has examples that illustrate this point?"

Kim, a brilliant marketing manager with a software company, answered. "Most companies with a customer loyalty program miss the mark. For instance, I have a membership card for a club at my local supermarket. When I reach the checkout line, the clerk asks if I have a club card, and since I do, I'm entitled to discounts and purchase points. What a mistake! First, consider this: what if there was a scanner at the store entrance, through which I would slide my card. Then, based on the information they have already gathered about me and my purchases using the RFM technique or some other Intimate Marketing tool I would receive special coupon offers based on items the supermarket predicts I will want to buy that day! The discounts could be for products I buy regularly, or—listen to this—big discounts for products I've never tried before. Instead of giving everyone the same discounts, the supermarket can tempt me to buy certain items, without anyone else knowing about it. Perhaps the product manufacturers themselves might be willing to subsidize these discounts.

"And maybe, when I enter the supermarket, the computer system can generate a personalized grocery list, as a reminder of items I typically purchase. How many times have you gone home and discovered you forgot to buy laundry soap? But the supermarket knows how often I buy it and can remind me!"

"I'm inviting you to take my place up here as lecturer Kim," said Elaine with appreciation. "A wonderful example, Kim! For something this good, you get a prize!" Elaine handed Kim a framed card, with the heading, *Do You Know Me?* and asked her to share the content with the group. It read:

Do You Know Me? Of course you do. I'm a 'nice' customer. I'm the one who never complains—no matter what kind of service I receive.

I'll go into a restaurant and sit quietly while the waitresses are gossiping about their boyfriends, instead of taking my order. Sometimes, others who come into the restaurant after me receive their meal before me, but I don't open my mouth. I don't complain either when the waitress says, "Oh, sorry, I'll have to put in another order for your meal." I simply wait.

I don't get upset when the waitress asks me, "Is everything okay?" and then leaves before I have a chance to answer. I don't grumble. Not ever. Nor do I make a scene over the fact that the bill brought to me belongs to the table next to me. I'm a nice customer.

But I'm also a customer that won't be back. "He who laughs last laughs best." And will I ever laugh, every time I see your big ads and commercials trying to get me to bring my business back to you—the ads that try to bring in more new customers, innocent suckers like I was.

Hey, look how much money you're throwing away now, eh? What a waste of time. Do you understand how easily you could have kept my business the first time, with just a little better service? A personal contact? A smile? A thank you? Basically, some real attention! You see, I want some intimacy with you. I want to feel you care.

It doesn't matter what business you're in. Maybe I've never even heard of you, and there's a good chance you've never heard of me, either. But with your business situation looking so bad, sales bottoming out, maybe it's because there are enough people like me who know you.

We are the customers who n-e-v-e-r return.

"Does someone else have other examples they'd like to share?" Elaine asked.

"Yes," said Michelle, a former teacher who had "moved the cheese"[1] and made a profitable career change from teaching to marketing management in her family's business. "I want to share an example to help everyone remember this rule, but not from the field of marketing. I have been seeing the same gynecologist for more than ten years. He knows everything about me from a medical standpoint, and most importantly, he remembers everything. When I see him, he doesn't write down a thing, but he remembers. It may be that he records things in his computer after I leave, but what is important to *me* is that he always remembers me, without looking at his terminal. He can see my eyeballs when we speak. I have rapport with him, and I trust him.

---

1   Phrase adapted from the book "Who Moved My Cheese" by Spencer Johnson which means adaptation to a new reality.

"Imagine if I had to tell my doctor my medical resume each time I saw him. As a former teacher, I can tell you that the art of remembering is the art of paying attention. In marketing, this is a winning formula. None of our customers care how much we know. They want to know how much we care. When we remember the 'little' things, they think we're great," Michelle concluded.

Elaine handed her a framed card too, and said, "Michelle, your comment was 100 percent correct. Thank you. I want very much for you all to learn the rest of the law of contact, so let's continue."

6. Pay a lot of attention to your first contact with a new customer.

In Intimate Marketing, your first contact is often the most critical. You will never have a second chance to make a good first impression. When customers meet you, they don't yet know that you're champions in Intimate Marketing. They don't know you will take good care of them. On the contrary, they may have many misgivings. Therefore, in the first few moments, it's worthwhile to show a new customer, in a variety of ways, that she or he has come to the right place.

Plan beforehand which kind of contact you will make with the customers when they engage with you. This is the first opportunity to strengthen your connection with them. Like a blind date where there is no mutual attraction, the chances of an eventual marriage are infinitely small indeed!

"Now for the seventh and final rule," Elaine said. She had the audience on the edge of their seats.

7. Check the effectiveness of these contacts.

From all this talk about contact and blind dates, you're liable to forget that we are dealing with a serious subject. The last rule of the Kama Sutra of marketing deals with the bottom line. Analyze the advantage gained with each contact. If you invest money, try to determine the rate of return on your investment.

You may learn that customers don't appreciate the fact that you sent them a 'happy birthday' card on their birthday. On the other hand, you may discover that contacts that cost nothing mean the most in terms of reinforcing Intimate Marketing and cultivating your relationship. If you sell face-to-face, there are plenty of ways to make your customers feel like kings when they come to your stores. One way to evaluate this is by doing a comparison.

Divide your preferred customers into two groups, and devote more attention to one group, using marketing contact. After a while, measure the results from this investment: did it increase their business activity with you? Did your customer 'share' increase? Did more customers from the second group leave? If so, you have clear proof that Intimate Marketing works!

By now, of course, you can see how the components of Intimate Marketing can overlap, and in accordance with 'customer lifetime value,' you would choose different kinds of contact. When you practice this system, you will enjoy steady progress in raising each customer's profitability.

Your marketing activities should be more advanced with your most valuable customers. Many companies operate on the '80/20 principle,' which says that 80 percent of the company's income is derived from purchases made by 20 percent of the customers. However, when we practice Intimate Marketing, we are interested in each customer's profitability. A survey conducted in the past found that about two-thirds of the large companies rank their customers by the volume of their purchases, not profitability.

When you become professionals with Intimate Marketing, you will be able to measure profitability too. Your business will begin to be managed, not by the '80/20 principle' but by the '40/250' rule. According to this rule, 40 percent of your customers create 250 percent of your profits!

Elaine paused for a few seconds to create a dramatic moment, and then continued.

You're no doubt asking how 250 percent is possible when the maximum is 100 percent, right? Here is an example. At the end of the 1980s a Swedish company determined that only 40 percent of their customers generated profit. In fact, they actually contributed 250 percent! Moreover, the company found that 5 percent of their most profitable customers created 150 percent of the profits. The most profitable customers simply covered the losses incurred by the rest of the customers!

To their surprise, the company's managers found that 10 percent of their customers were responsible for reducing the profits by half, and two customers from that 10 percent belonged to their key accounts, those who were buying the most! And you know the myth of "we cannot lose a big customer," don't you?

This company, a world-leading brand for products and services in the area of industrial heating technology and resistance materials, learned to measure not only temperature but also each customer's contribution to profit or loss, and as a result, are now able to eliminate the customers who drain profits and invest in creative contacts with those more profitable customers.

"Now," said Elaine, "let's evaluate your creativity. Let's combine the seven 'laws of contact' with the marketing paradigm of the 21st century—the Internet. Let's suppose you want to improve communication and contact between a chain of electronics stores and their customers. Breaking into groups of three, I'd like you to come up with three useful ideas through which the chain can apply Intimate Marketing so that the chain not only benefits, but also of course, so do the customers. Let's take fifteen minutes to brainstorm."

The groups appeared to enjoy their brainstorming session. Sex jokes were being traded as well among some of the groups that had forgotten to behave in a politically correct manner. *That's what happens when you mix marketing with Kama Sutra,* Elaine thought wryly. *On the other hand, when people are laughing, their brains are working creatively.*

Elaine asked for a volunteer from each group to summarize their most dazzling ideas aloud. Meanwhile she listed them on flip charts, taping them one after another on the meeting room walls. Most were ideas that any company could adopt:

- *Let customers order repair and parts replacement services through the Internet.*
- *Enable customers to download user manuals from the net, according to their purchases.*
- *Create customer forums among people who bought similar products.*
- *Offer automatic service reminders for maintenance dates.*
- *Have downloadable coupons and appropriate personal discounts for the customer based on needs.*
- *Receive recommendations for improvements and new products.*
- *Send emails to the call center to have them call the customer back (no waiting on hold) at a specified time.*
- *Sell insurance for appliances.*
- *Use Facebook*
- *Request that they fill out a feedback form.*
- *Send them a personal e-zine (electronic magazine).*
- *Request that they turn in complaints on the worst part of the service that they received. Strongly recommend that, in order to prevent the*

same thing happening to someone else, they make recommendations
for how to improve in the future.

Elaine looked with satisfaction at the groups and said, "It seems you all need a little contact with some cake and coffee, so let's take a short break, and afterwards, we'll introduce one of the most important kinds of contact."

Elaine was pleased with herself. She had succeeded in getting through the first part of the meeting without any thoughts of Daniel interfering. Only now did the thoughts return, crowding her mind. Her eyes followed Sammy, but it looked like he was leaving. The break ended. In order to demonstrate her point, Elaine began dramatically by showing a slide with twenty large question marks. While doing this, the latecomers found their seats. To her pleasant surprise, Sammy was among them.

"Now we'll learn about building an Intimate Marketing relationship using questionnaires," Elaine began.

One of the most effective means for strengthening Intimate Marketing is based on questionnaires. In my various lectures to managers and marketers, I use examples from companies who sent selected customers a questionnaire with just ten questions to get at issues like consumer habits, personal details, etc. Then I ask those present what they think the response rate was. Usually, their answers range from 5-20 percent. Here comes the first surprise: people love to answer questionnaires. There are cases where the response rate was as high as 50 percent. How and why does this happen?

It turns out that the average customer, yours included, likes to feel that someone values her opinion. Your customers will want to express themselves if they believe that the result will be better service. Since both sides have the same goal—a close and better relationship —soliciting feedback makes perfect sense.

In Intimate Marketing, you ask your customers what they like or dislike about your products and services, and what they would like you to continue doing, or stop doing. The questionnaire is an outstanding opportunity to improve your marketing intimacy, to really get to know some of your customers, at least those who decide to answer your questions honestly. The questionnaire you send is designed to create a personal dialogue with each and every customer. The personal details are stored in your customer database, and in applying the results, you can design marketing offers for each customer, relating to each one in the most efficient and appropriate manner.

You will notice that not everyone will respond, but this doesn't mean they don't want contact. At least for the moment, assume they were not able to fill out the questionnaire and perhaps never even received it. Those who did not answer can be approached at least one more time at a later date, or even with a different method. Everyone responds to different approaches. Don't forget that we are talking about Intimate Marketing, which is based on taking the appropriate action to attract and keep customers. Sending out questionnaires is only one approach. You must find the best way to solicit customer feedback, remembering that Intimate Marketing is based largely on continuous dialogue.

"Could you share with us some tips to design the right questionnaire?" asked someone.

"Sure. Here are some tips from my own experience," Elaine said.

First, write down the ultimate goal for your survey, as well as how the customer will benefit. Define this as precisely as possible. Remember that the more the customer believes filling out the questionnaire will benefit him or her, the greater your chances of getting back a detailed response. Don't forget to note the questionnaire's goal in the introduction and how the company will apply the results. In some cases, it might be wise to share how the survey recipients were selected and why your research effort is so important.

In most cases, if you don't do an electronic questionnaire, enclosing a self-addressed, stamped, return envelope with the questionnaire, and noting a deadline for completion will boost your response rate. Today, many companies want to save money and use only web-based feedback forms, but you should remember that there are customers who prefer to do it the old-school way, and they do not give their feedback online. The voice of your customer is very important and you should focus your efforts on getting everybody's feedback!

Not every questionnaire you administer will measure customer satisfaction, but measuring customer satisfaction is very important in Intimate Marketing, particularly for strengthening the connection with your customers. Your customers' responses, fed into an information system in a way that facilitates analysis and cross-referencing, will help you improve your customer service immeasurably. For example, you may want to isolate all customers who made less than three purchases in the last year, and rated your service as a 4 on a 7-point scale, so you can target specific offers to them.

"Could you share with us some tips on how to get them to respond?" asked John, a brand manager from Procter & Gamble.

"That's a great question! Who might like to suggest some answers?" replied Elaine. She recorded their answers on the flip chart:

...Promise a special gift to everyone who fills out the questionnaire.
...Attach a stamped, self-addressed envelope.
...Attach a gift to the questionnaire itself as a token of appreciation (perhaps a discount coupon or a gift certificate).

...Announce an unexpected benefit to the customer as a result of filling out the questionnaire.

...Invest the time and make the necessary effort in the survey design. Format can make a significant difference in the response rate. It should be easy to follow and simple to complete.

...Enclose some kind of gimmick in the envelope, or a one-dollar bill.

...Offer a lottery ticket to those who fill out the questionnaire where there is one grand prize and several small ones, so those with little faith in lotteries will comply for the chance to win at least a small prize.

...Make sure the questions are arranged so that the more intimate questions will be asked near the end.

...Attach a 'president's personal letter' to the customer asking for his help and emphasizing the importance of hearing his honest answers.

...Phrase questions clearly and concisely.

...Take care not to repeat questions, unless they are worded differently and are designed to check for consistent answers from the respondents.

...Let them know in advance that a survey will be arriving (in some cases) saying, "next week you will receive a questionnaire...." This increases their level of curiosity and presumably the response rate.

...Send a second request if they don't respond the first time.

...Give them as many ways to respond as possible—by phone, email, web site, or snail mail.

Elaine added her own thoughts:

...A note to consider: the more non-respondents there are, the greater the likelihood you don't know your customers well enough. If you don't find out who they are, it's almost impossible to apply Intimate Marketing principles.

...Receiving answers to questionnaires is an important step in strengthening the Intimate Marketing relationship between a company and its customers, and also helps identify trends and marketing opportunities. Here is an exercise you can do yourselves: If you have

sent a questionnaire to your customers in the past, check to see how many respondents are also your most loyal customers. If you find a high correlation, that is that those who responded are your best customers, you can develop strategies to strengthen your relationship with the non-respondents.

…It should be noted further that those who respond and list complaints are excellent customers! Submitting a complaint is a message that the customer believes you are listening and willing and able to resolve it. Otherwise, she or he wouldn't bother but would simply take their business elsewhere. Many researchers have proven that customers who got their complaints resolved are ultimately the company's most loyal customers—more loyal than those who never complained. In summary, always encourage your customers to speak their minds. If they feel you listen, they will value the relationship with you.

"We have fifteen minutes left for questions. Does someone want to comment?" asked Elaine.

A manager of a Japanese car dealership said, "Sometimes, I want to get answers to questions, but I don't want to ask my customer outright. What do you recommend?"

Elaine answered, "Domo arigato," which is the Japanese phrase meaning 'thank you very much.' "That's a very good comment. At times, you want your customers to answer an important question, but you want to camouflage it, in order to get a more honest response. This is perhaps one of the best applications for questionnaires, because you can draw out what you really want with a series of other questions. I'll give you an example.

"You are interested in finding out when your customer is considering trading his car in for a new one, so you can offer him a deal at the appropriate time. In doing so, you can pose questions that will also help you with general marketing."

She listed five questions on the board:

1. *What three things do you like most about your car?*
2. *What, if anything, would you like to change about it?*
3. *What kind of car does your best friend own?*
4. *In your opinion, how long should someone keep a new Japanese car, considering depreciation, maintenance, etc., as opposed to buying another new car?*
5. *In retrospect, if you had it to do over again, what car would you have purchased?*
   ___ *Same car*
   ___ *Other car*

She finished writing and then explained, "Questions number one and number two help you identify customer-perceived advantages and disadvantages—things that might influence their next purchase. Question number three sometimes helps identify ambitions, since people tend to adopt a lifestyle similar to that of their close friends. Of course, if the good friend has an inferior car, this question won't add value. On the other hand, if the friend *does* have an inferior car, you can enlist a help from your customer in selling *the friend* a car like *your customer's* by applying the strategy of asking for referrals. This is another example of increasing your customer's 'lifetime value'!

"Question number four is a basic question for predicting when the customer will consider making a trade-in, and question number five provides more information about his priorities and your potential competition for his next purchase. All of this information is useful, not only in terms of meeting each customer's immediate needs, but also for general customer preferences.

"Okay, before I give you an important mission, let me quote Robert Sternberg, an American psychologist and psychometrician. Sternberg said, "Passion is the quickest to develop and the quickest to fade. Intimacy develops more slowly, and commitment more gradually still." Now, for the next session, please write a questionnaire to send to your current customers, and another one to send to a select group of former customers. Goodbye, and have a great, intimate day."

Elaine closed her session and looked over at Sammy seated across from her looking quite interested. After gathering his things, he approached her. "Elaine, you are really a great speaker," he said enthusiastically, and then he asked when the next meeting would be. Elaine answered him warmly, all the while searching his face for some sign as to whether or not he knew what had happened with Daniel and trying to decide if she should ask him if he knew.

Chapter 9

It's About Love...

To her relief, Sammy volunteered to walk Elaine to the parking lot. When they were just a few feet from her car, Sammy's cell phone rang.

"Danny!" he said. "Hey, do you know where I am right now? I'm in Manhattan, standing right next to your princess!" A few seconds later, Elaine saw his face redden slightly. *It must be something Daniel said*, she thought. Sammy quickly finished the call.

"Did something happen?" Elaine asked, but Sammy avoided answering her. "Is he okay? Can I reach him somewhere?"

Sammy was slow in answering. "Elaine, I like you very much. I think you need to talk to Daniel yourself," was all he said, and Elaine experienced a bad taste in her mouth. Something was happening...

Sammy left her, but not before lavishing her with praise about her lecture. She knew he was keeping something from her, but she didn't know what to do. If there was bad news on the horizon, maybe it was better to postpone hearing it. Maybe it would pass in a few hours. Maybe Daniel would call and say everything had worked out, and they would listen to music together as they had planned two days ago. What could have gone wrong with him? Did he have some health problems?

Elaine drove home deep in gloomy thought. All she wanted now was a little quiet. Her home was the best place she could think of at the moment.

She walked into the apartment and saw the message light on her answering machine. Why didn't he call her cell phone? It was a message from Daniel, wanting her to call him. But she decided to shower and make a cup of tea first. She could hear the apologetic tone in his voice. Something had definitely happened, and she wanted to put off finding out what it was, give herself a few minutes or hours to continue in the sweet illusion that all was well....

Elaine stood for a while at the kitchen sink, letting warm water run over her fingers and taking longer than necessary to wash the two dirty cups and three plates. Her thoughts would not let her rest. She still couldn't decide whether she should call Daniel back and, if so, when? On the other hand, she wondered if she should just wait for him to call her back again.

A sharp ring from the phone interrupted her thoughts. Her heart jumped, but she sprang up to answer it with firm steps. It was Sammy. He was on his way back to the farm and apologized for bothering her.

"No, Sammy, you're not bothering me," Elaine reassured him, and in her heart she was happy to have a diversion from her worries over Daniel, not to mention a reason to tie up the phone line.

"Tell me, Elaine, which business fields can apply Intimate Marketing?" he asked.

Elaine smiled to herself. "Listen, Sammy, that's at least a half-hour lecture. Are you sure you have time?"

"Sure," he said, and Elaine went into lecturing mode once again.

"Intimate Marketing depends upon marketing for an extended time in order to create ongoing intimate relationships with your customers. So, it's especially appropriate for businesses, products, and services with an interest in continuing activity," she began with great patience. "The main point is that every business based on repeating sales over time is appropriate for applying the Intimate Marketing principles; and if you look around, you will discover most businesses are appropriate.

"Even if one type of business doesn't match all the criteria, partial use of Intimate Marketing principles is still worthwhile. Do you want to hear about fields that are really suitable for Intimate Marketing? For example, the distribution of dietary or organic-food products, or any other food products for which there is demand by a specific market segment can apply Intimate Marketing principles quite successfully. In addition, product and service providers for animals, the elderly, or for babies, financial services for managers and business people, insurance, cleaning and maintenance services, medical and nursing, all sort of subscriptions, theater and the arts, credit card companies, and sports and gaming clubs would also find it advantageous. Do you want more examples?" Elaine asked.

"Don't overdo it, I got the idea," Sammy admitted. "Tell me—who invented this approach to marketing? Don't tell me it was you."

Elaine laughed at the compliment. "I only wish, Sammy. A friend of mine, international speaker Gil Peretz, coined the concept. But the truth is, I really feel as if I invented it. You know what? I'll send you an article right now that I wrote about the history of Intimate Marketing. Give me two minutes and it is in your inbox, okay? Thanks for coming to my session and please give a hug to Lynn."

* * *

When he arrived home about forty minutes later, Sammy made a cup of coffee in the small kitchen and sat down to read the article Elaine had sent. While his eyes scanned the words, his thoughts turned toward Elaine. *What a wonderful lady, and what a fool Danny is for not understanding what he may be losing if he does follow through with his intentions. I should try to reach him on the phone, quickly....but then again, in his confused state, perhaps it's better to give him some space; he won't listen to me anyway.*

When was Intimate Marketing born? read the headline. Sammy was increasingly curious. As he read, he felt that he was absorbing the words with surprising speed. He couldn't remember any course in his earlier years in which he was this interested in the material!

Intimate Marketing is based on accumulated knowledge about marketing principles used over the last hundred years. We could say that its birth coincided with the development of the catalog industry in the U.S. The Sears catalog, for example, first appeared back in 1897, and a mere five years later at the turn of the century it was bringing in annual mail-order sales of $50 million!

Much of the technique for maintaining ongoing customer attraction is based on the information accumulated since the beginning of the Book of the Month Club in 1926. Actually, most customer clubs today are patterned after one of two kinds of clubs which laid the foundation for the industry: the Book of the Month Club and the airlines' Frequent Flyer program.

Parallel to the development of direct marketing through catalogs and direct mail, were a number of trends in the world of consumer marketing. First, investment grew in mass publicity. More and more companies poured millions into creating advertisements for brand strengthening—to create a more favorable image, educate the public, and supply product information, all by emphasizing the customer advantages of product use.

As the marketing network grew, and the battle for the customer's business became tougher, a surprising new weapon was introduced: the coupon. Within a short time, the coupon became an effective means of reminding the customer which product and brand to buy. When customers entered the supermarket with coupons in hand, the likelihood of their buying those particular brands was far greater. The companies distributing coupons gained priority attention (if only temporarily) for their brands over those of their competitors, and store owners enjoyed the benefits of people coming in to redeem a coupon and buying other (impulse) items at the same time.

The Internet changed the world. Instead of the old coupons you might be a customer of Groupon, and every business can have a relationship with millions of unique customers if it adopts the Intimate Marketing culture and uses the amazing services the Net can offer to profit from your customers.

Intimate Marketing, based on gathering and analyzing as much information as possible about customer buying habits, is combined with today's sophisticated technology to create more effective and profitable relationships with your customers.

Sammy stopped reading, and thought about how similar Intimate Marketing was to ongoing attraction in love. He took a piece of paper, drew a heart at its center, and inside the heart he wrote: *How to Keep a Relationship Forever*. He began to record his thoughts on his drawing and adding arrows pointing from the heart.

Don't betray your partner. Don't take anything for granted. Continue to invest even after the first thrill is gone. Invest. Be friends. Surprise your partner. Really listen. Yield. Forgive. Be interested in your partner. Remember. Love your partner. Develop and grow together. True partnership. Trust. Rapport.

Sammy enjoyed fantasizing, and suddenly he stopped and realized what he had written was relevant not only for preserving his relationship with Lynn, his wife whom he dearly loved, but also appropriate to marketing. *Marketing really is an intimate process,* thought Sammy, pleased with his creation. *At the first opportunity, I'll show it to Elaine,* he mused. *It's all about love.*

* * *

That evening, Daniel sat in his small apartment, slurping noodles from his coffee mug. The hands of the clock were quickly moving to seven-thirty. He knew that in a few minutes, Gail Shannon, the beautiful flight attendant and former girlfriend with whom he had once woven the rosiest dreams in the world, would be knocking on his door. When was that? A year and a half ago? Two? At which point she suddenly decided she needed a time-out, wanted to live in another country and meet new people... and even hinted about a young, interesting and charming millionaire from Canada who was making moves in her direction.

It had taken Daniel several long months to recover from Gail's sudden departure. With dulled eyes he would go to work, trying to avoid people who knew them as a couple, as well as the flight attendants. Before boarding a plane, he would first verify that Gail and her million-dollar smile were not on duty. When he finally heard that she had indeed left the U.S. and her job at International Airlines for Canada (presumably) to meet her millionaire, he had hoped that *she*, at least, was happy.

That's why the phone call yesterday was so surprising. Gail in the flesh—heartwarming and happy, with that voice that made his heart stop. Suddenly, there she was, so close and touchable. His Gail, the gorgeous love of his life, was back in the States and wanted to see him.

He was not in a rush to meet her. He knew Elaine was waiting, a woman no less beautiful and intelligent than Gail—someone who perhaps truly cherished him, and surely wouldn't abandon him for a millionaire. On the other hand, how well did he really know Elaine? *We've never spoken, Elaine and I, about what we each want for the future. Maybe she's planning a new life for herself somewhere else, just like Gail.* In the end, he couldn't resist the temptation to see Gail.

Daniel was excited at the prospect, as well as curious about her life in Canada. Maybe he also felt flattered that he was the first man she had decided to see upon returning. *But what do I say to Elaine?* He knew she was probably planning for them to get together, waiting, thinking about him.

Gail was pretty determined to come back to him, or at least it appeared that way. "But what happened in

Canada? Where did your millionaire friend go to?" Daniel had asked on the phone, very curious to hear what her response would be. But yesterday, it seemed Gail wasn't ready to share any details. She was more interested in how *he* was doing, how her friends at the airline were, and whether or not he was seeing anyone these days. Daniel tried to avoid giving a straight answer. Suddenly, he didn't know exactly what to say, since he had only known Elaine for a few days. He preferred to keep quiet about her.

Gail arrived on time, full of cheerful self-assurance. She kissed him, wafting that perfume that used to drive him crazy for her. She knew how to please him. They had dated for three years, a long time by all accounts. Gail had hardly changed. She was still stunning, no doubt causing every passerby on the street to look twice. She was thirty-one, slender and attractive, smart, and full of ambition. He could see himself walking down the aisle with her, surrounded by members of both of their families, all of them proud of the match. But was that really the right step? There was something fickle about Gail; hadn't she jumped at the opportunity for a new life without him? Why did he still feel something for her? Daniel offered her coffee, which she gladly accepted.

Gail wasn't overly talkative. She gazed at him, held his hand, and stroked his cheek, his eyes, his eyebrows… Her touch was soft and gentle, but also determined. She wanted to go to bed with him that evening; Daniel knew her well enough to figure that out. Would he be able to withstand the temptation? Or, more to the point, *how* would he withstand her?

The telephone rang, interrupting his thoughts. He parted from Gail and went to answer it. Elaine! Finally she had gathered the courage to call him. Daniel felt more confused than ever.

He knew he owed Elaine an explanation, an apology, an honest talk, but right now was certainly not the time. Tiger pounced on Gail, and she shrieked loudly. Elaine, hearing the shriek on her end, was quiet. She finally said in a choked voice, "I can hear you're busy now," and hung up.

* * *

Tears filled Elaine's blue eyes and a lump closed her throat. Once more she felt that huge loneliness, the disappointment, the bitter taste of abandonment. Again, she knew she would have to gather her strength, her wits, and her loved ones around her, to get over the short but intense romantic relationship of the past week. *Why does this always happen to me?* she wondered, but only hot, wet tears came in response. The phone rang, but she didn't answer. Elaine felt her personal world crashing down around her, and she had neither desire nor strength to carry on a heartfelt conversation with anyone.

"A business call," Daniel explained to Gail, trying to make the short, abrupt phone conversation seem reasonable. Gail accepted the explanation without question. She was so sure of herself and her hold on Daniel, so confident that she could get him back if she cared to, that he felt he had almost no choice, other than to move forward with Gail's plans.

"The millionaire turned out to be a complete loser," Gail said of her life in Canada. "It was very tempting to be a part of his life with the huge house, with the private pool and tennis courts, stables, jeep, and private plane. But we had absolutely nothing to talk about. All day he was away from home and he expected me to play the sweet little wife at weekend meetings with his rich friends. I dumped him pretty quickly and without regrets, but I felt like staying in Canada a while longer. I really liked the country—amazingly green, lots of water and wildflowers everywhere.

"I took some courses in French and business administration, got to know a lot of people, and at one point I even thought I might settle down there. But as soon as I started thinking about it seriously, I would remember all my friends, especially you, Daniel, and the talks and laughs we had shared together, all the things others could never understand. I got so homesick that I knew as soon as I finished my courses I'd return. But I was too embarrassed to call people and tell them, so I decided to just show up."

Daniel looked at her and tried to sort out his thoughts about Gail, and about her story. It was true he had been crazy about her; he would have married her in a minute under any conditions. He would have flown to the moon with her. But two years had passed since then, two hard years of thinking and maturing. He now knew other women; he had met a wonderful woman—Elaine. It seemed impossible that all this would count for nothing just because Gail suddenly reappeared.

"Gail, I'm awfully tired," he said abruptly. "Maybe we can continue our get-together another day? I'm going through a really pressured time at work. I need to sleep normal hours; otherwise, I'm going to screw up some important international projects."

"Too bad," Gail said. "I had some other plans for us, and I wanted to tell you about the incredible job I got. But okay, we can postpone it for another time." She hoped Daniel would get curious and ask, but he was deep in thought. Gail didn't try to force herself on him. She just smiled sweetly, kissed him slyly on the forehead, picked up her coat and shoulder bag, blew another kiss at him, and left. "We'll talk tomorrow," she called back through the door.

Gail's perfume hovered in the room for a long while after she left. Only after it faded did Daniel dare dial Elaine's telephone number. He fervently hoped she would answer, and give him a chance to explain, but the phone rang and rang, until finally the voice mail picked up the call. He decided not to leave a message.

Daniel was disappointed. He didn't want to hurt or lose Elaine and certainly not this fast. He didn't know what to do. In his imagination, he paged through his three years with Gail. They had never fought. He had loved her greatly. They looked good together. Maybe he really was making a mistake, and he could simply forgive her and pick up right where they had left off.

In the end, he decided just to go to sleep. No day was so bad it couldn't be fixed with a nap. The best bridge between despair and hope was a good night's sleep.

Maybe in the morning things would be clearer.

Chapter 10

Forever Faithful

*T*he ringing alarm clock started Elaine from her sleep. *If people were meant to pop out of bed, we'd all sleep in toasters.* She woke up with a start, and then she realized that she had slept for ten full hours. The events of the previous day flooded her mind, but without yesterday's sharp pain. *A familiar process,* she smiled to herself. *Wounded, yet moving on.* She had too much to do today to be fretting over 'Daniel the Deadbeat.' At ten this morning, she was scheduled for a telephone interview with a New York radio station, speaking about 'The Ten Laws to Prevent Customer Betrayal.'

At exactly nine-fifty-four the phone rang. The interviewer introduced himself to Elaine and told her not to be nervous. He explained that they would be on the air very shortly and asked her to stand by until he introduced her. He opened the program by referring to Elaine as the Doctor Ruth of marketing, and then asked her to share with the listeners ten marketing principles to prevent customer betrayal.

Law Number One is the Law of Paranoia. *Andy Grove, former chairman and CEO of Intel, said that only the paranoids survive. Well,* *my advice is to adopt his motto. You should operate in constant fear that your customers will be stolen from you. This constructive fear should motivate you to monitor the market carefully, and never rest on your laurels. Everyone has competitors, you know—and your best customers are their best potential customers. The competition would be happy to entice them to leave you.*

Forget the phrase 'my customer,' and instead adopt the concept 'my customer for the moment.' The challenge you face is to stretch this moment for as long as possible. You have no time to focus on such an assignment? Too busy to hunt for new customers? Well, your competitors are busy at work on this, and if you don't devote some time this week to this effort, you'll have a lot of time in the future to think, after they steal your customers...

Law Number Two is the Law of Constant Contact. *Give yourself points each time you visit a customer face to face or make some kind of direct contact with them. Surprise a customer with a visit. Send them funny postcards from your vacation spot, and so on. Award 'circulation points' to employees who pop out of the office periodically to see customers. Then offer a prize to the worker who accumulates the most points. If you take these extra measures, chances are fewer that your customers will betray you.*

"Okay. Paranoia and constant contact. What else?" asked the host.

Law Number Three—The Law of Non-Stop Learning. *For true professionals, school is never finished. Just as you must study to stay abreast of new developments in your field, you also have to study to stay on top of your customers, their businesses, their products, their competition, etc. Call your customer's sales department (of course you can use an assumed name) and request information about their services. When you read the newspapers, or when you're on the net, keep an eye out for information about your customer's businesses, market, or* *industries. The more you know about their world, the more you can help them succeed. This will help you stay ahead of the competition.*

Law Number Four—The Law of Love. *Sales and customer service are useful tools for attracting and ensuring endless love. Attract your veteran customers on a permanent basis, and look for creative and surprising ways to keep them happy. I developed seven laws of contact, which you can download from my website. Don't give your customers reasons to dump you.*

Law Number Five—The Law of Involvement. *Involve your customers in the work you do for them. Ask for their help; consult with them regularly. The more you communicate and share ideas with each other, the more blended the line that divides you. You can even establish a 'customer council,' to meet from time to time and discuss ways to develop better solutions for service improvement. The more involved customers become, and the more they invest emotionally, the harder it will be for them to leave you.*

"If you can't beat 'em, meet 'em," added the host wryly.

Law Number Six—The Law of Celebration. *Look for opportunities to celebrate events in your customers' lives. Send them a cake with a single candle in celebration of completing one year of business with you. Competitors will have a hard time enticing a satisfied customer with whom you've recently celebrated success.*

"Cake it 'till you make it," laughed the host.

Law Number Seven—The Law of Guerilla Marketing. *Call your staff to a special meeting to brainstorm how you can steal your competitor's customers. Don't be afraid to speak provocatively, because this will give people permission to aim high by raising ideas they wouldn't dare offer if the meeting was more reserved. Before ending the meeting, decide what to* try immediately and what should be delayed for the future. But this is just the beginning. The next part is even more gripping. Think about how you might respond if your competitor copies what you're doing. Prepare your anti-theft weapons, so that all your forces are ready for an enemy challenge.

Law Number Eight—The Law of Semester Reports. Similar to report cards students receive after each semester, or like the performance evaluation meetings for employees, conduct customer meetings to summarize the close of a period. Emphasize that your goal is to summarize the period, to evaluate what occurred, to hear their comments and concerns and, lastly, to discuss joint expectations for the upcoming period and the longer-term future. If you make this meeting an integral part of your contact plan, you will have created a commitment to keep in close contact with the customer. It is always better to hear customer feedback directly than to discover a customer has deserted you because he had no opportunity to express himself. Holding periodic meetings also helps keep the customer committed by making an emotional investment. A customer who is emotionally involved will not be in a hurry to leave.

"Elaine, your laws are very important. Since we have one more minute, please tell us the last two laws," said the host.

Law Number Nine—The Law of Diplomacy. As you succeed in turning your customers into active diplomats, the opportunities will only increase.

"How do you do that?" asked the interviewer.

"Very simple," Elaine answered. "Ask one of your customers to conduct a lecture for your staff about his company and products. Look for ways to use your customers as honorary ambassadors at different events, and in short, help them succeed personally and form strong social bonds with them."

Law Number Ten—The Law of Deterrence. *You can reduce customer theft by becoming regular customers of your customers. This law is applicable especially to firms engaged in business-to-business services. By making the customer understand that if he betrays you, it will cost him more than he realizes, he is more motivated to remain as your customer.*

In summary, the goal of these ten laws is to keep you from feeling indifferent and from making excuses like "that's how it is in our business," or "customer turnover is a fact of life," and so on, and to get you to invest in managing your competition. If you start applying even just a few of these laws for a short time with a small—but important—number of your customers, you will soon see how effective it is for preventing customer attrition.

"Thank you for sharing your 'Ten Laws of Betrayal' prevention with us. We might adapt and use some of these in our personal lives as well," said the host.

Elaine hung up the phone, satisfied with her interview, and rose from her chair to refill her coffee. The doorbell rang, causing her to detour on her way to the kitchen. When she opened the door, a friendly messenger in a motorcycle helmet, greeted her, holding a giant tropical bouquet of seven beautiful birds of paradise, greenery, and willow branches, with an attached letter in a purple envelope.

Her heart skipped a beat. She took the flowers and the envelope, having no doubt about who had sent it. Her hands trembled. But she proceeded first to the kitchen to get that cup of coffee, debating whether or not she should even open the envelope.

Elaine, Daniel began his letter, *I decided to write you because I was afraid you wouldn't want to talk to me—and also because maybe I wouldn't explain myself very well face to* face. Two years ago, I had a girlfriend whom I loved very much. We were even contemplating marriage, but she suddenly left me and moved to Canada. And now...

Elaine continued skimming the pages, reading the words, feeling each one like a dart piercing her heart as though she were a target at some cheap bar.

After she finished reading, she went into the kitchen, lit a match, and set fire to the envelope, getting a small amount of pleasure from seeing the purple pages turn to brown-black ash before her eyes. She was suddenly struck by the way her professional and personal life intertwined. *Maybe there really is no true loyalty in life. Maybe it doesn't matter what I do. Sooner or later, someone is going to ruin it for me. Even if I invest time in making myself attractive to someone and really love him, in the end, people are only interested in looking out for Number One. Maybe that's the way I should be too.*

Elaine decided to show Daniel what a small world it is.

She went to her desk, dialed 1-800-I-FLY-SWA, and asked to be transferred to the manager of the Frequent Flyer program of Southwest Airlines. A pleasant feminine voice answered. Elaine introduced herself and asked for details on how to participate in the Rapid Rewards® program. "Welcome, Elaine—you will find that we are ready to offer you the best experience and service you've ever seen," responded the manager. "By the way, my name is Gail Shannon, and if you need anything..."

Epilogue

Elaine browsed through her iPad and suddenly lowered her head. Thoughts were running through her mind with lightening speed: *In Intimate Marketing, like in love, the other side can betray you—even if you do everything you should.*

On the other hand, there's no substitute for doing everything you can. If you really love someone, invest in them, pamper them, and make your dreams come true together. Surprise your partner, talk things over, and yield in an argument. Get to know them, ask, remember, accept and give, walk a mile in the other person's shoes (or slippers). Don't take anything for granted, be friends, keep confidences, be involved and listen, change together, be loyal—and who knows—maybe it's possible to apply all this to something besides business...

Afterword

Do you have a 'love letter?'

Yes, I admit it! I *love* to get feedback.

I love to hear opinions after I speak as a keynote speaker at international conferences.

I love to learn from others.

So, if you have feedback, or if you just feel like sharing with me what you liked or didn't like about the book, what concepts you will apply, or any other thoughts related to Intimate Marketing, please send me a 'love letter.'

Please visit our website at www.IntimateMarketing.com, or send your letter, along with a few details about yourself, to gil@gilperetz.com

Gil Peretz

International speaker **Gil Peretz** is one of the world's leading authorities on communication and sales training. With more than 25 years of experience, Gil has coached and trained thousands of CEOs, entrepreneurs, sales experts, coaches, political leaders, and diplomats.

Since 1986, Gil has delivered more than 2,600 keynote addresses, presentations, and seminars. He is considered a results-driven trainer covering a range of topics including communication, presentation skills, whole-brain selling, negotiation, intimate marketing, and training for impact.

Gil has helped a wide range of organizations unleash their sales teams' potential. Global Fortune 500 companies engage Gil for their keynote addresses, breakout sessions, and to coach executives on their presentations. His delivery is "fast, simple, and amazing." Getting Gil's secrets into your organization will be a fast process; it will be a very simple process to implement; and the results are amazing.

Gil's clients include international organizations such as Microsoft, Motorola, Coca-Cola, IBM, Allergan, Merck, Teva, Pfizer, Philip Morris International, Swiss International Air Lines, HP, Hertz, Orange, Ericsson, Hilton, British American Tobacco, Manpower, Dun & Bradstreet,

M-systems, Comverse, Peugeot, Citroen, Lee Cooper, Delta, and many more.

As a highly respected member of the American National Speakers Association, Gil has been invited to deliver his *"unforgettable presentations"* many times across the globe at conventions and conferences attended by thousands of participants.

Since 2009, Gil has been invited to deliver his seminars about *Obama's effective secrets of communication* and the ways in which they can be utilized for marketing presentations, sales calls, and even in education.

Gil is considered a high-energy, virtuoso intimate speaker with rare presentation talents and a special ability to bond with any audience. Participants at his lectures feel that he speaks to each of them, individually, as if it were an intimate talk. The participants always leave with ideas for immediate implementation and, no less important, with a sense that they have taken part in a special intellectual and emotional experience.

Gil has been teaching "Marketing 101" and "Sharpening Your Presentation and Speech Skills" at the University of Tel-Aviv's Faculty of Management – The Leon Recanati Graduate School of Business Administration.

Gil is coauthor of *Obama's Secrets: How to Speak and Communicate with Power and a Little Magic.*

To explore the possibilities of bringing the power of Gil Peretz to your organization, please contact gil@gilperetz.com

www.gilperetz.com

www.IntimateMarketing.com

Recommendations from Linkedin ®

"Gil is an exciting and charismatic speaker. He manages to produce a rare blend of practical management and business principles laced with humor, memorable examples and intelligent wit. As a professional presenter and trainer myself, I very much enjoyed his lecture series and gained personal benefit from his special approach."

"Gil is a brilliant speaker. His presentations are both informative and fun. As Gil so successfully preaches to convey complex messages in simple terms, all that needs to be said is, "don't miss Gil's presentations"!"

"Gil is an outstanding keynote speaker with exceptional presentation skills. The crowd was hypnotized! Gil uses innovative tools to convey his key messages thus ensuring active participation on the part of his audience and thorough assimilation of the aforesaid messages. Gil understands the cultural difference among international audiences and has shown the ability to carefully craft the appropriate messaging and tools to use upon each separate engagement."

"Gil helped me optimize my presentation to a very high level. His open and constructive critique, in a very pleasant yet precise manner was extremely beneficial for me in my preparation before a large audience presentation."

"Gil is an energetic speaker who embodies forward thinking. Gil's approach to issues is straight to the point, no-nonsense, and infused with humor and ease. If you are looking for someone to inspire your organization and open the door to better communication inside out, Gil delivers!"

"Gil Perez is a great speaker. I have had the pleasure of attending a number of his presentations at various events. I was impressed and highly inspired. I will strongly recommend Gil as a consultant for seminars on presentation/communication skills."

"Gil is a talented, creative, visionary entrepreneur with energy and discipline to match his vision. Not only does he have great ideas – he knows how to bring those ideas into reality! If you're looking for a guy who can deliver the goods, Gil is your man. I recommend him highly."

"I have hired Gil to guide me through a 'once in a life time' presentation to the management of one of the biggest FMCG (Fast Moving Consumer Goods) companies in the world. Gil helped me transformed a boring, data based presentation to an emotions-burst of the esteemed audience. Gil's outside the box ideas together with an excellent understanding of how to influence the audience is highly appreciated!"

"Gil deserves every possible superlative that's out there. He is one of the most professional business persons I have come across. I would recommend Gil for any type of project related to personal training, coaching and business advisory."

* * *

To explore the possibilities of bringing Gil Peretz to your organization, contact gil@gilperetz.com